Office of Factory Inspector Illinois

First Special Report of the Factory Inspectors of Illinois

On Small-pox in the Tenement House Sweat-Shops of Chicago

Office of Factory Inspector Illinois

First Special Report of the Factory Inspectors of Illinois
On Small-pox in the Tenement House Sweat-Shops of Chicago

ISBN/EAN: 9783337151676

Printed in Europe, USA, Canada, Australia, Japan

Cover: Foto ©Suzi / pixelio.de

More available books at **www.hansebooks.com**

STATE OF ILLINOIS,
OFFICE OF FACTORY INSPECTOR,
247 W. POLK ST.

CHICAGO, July, 1, 1894.

HON JOHN P. ALTGELD,
  Governor of Illinois.

DEAR SIR:—I have the honor to submit herewith a special report on tenement house manufacture in Chicago during the small-pox epidemic of 1894, according to your instruction of June 25th.

Yours very truly,

FLORENCE KELLEY,

State Factory Inspector.

SPECIAL REPORT

ON

Small-Pox in the Tenement House Sweat-Shops of Chicago, 1894.

The work of the State Factory Inspectors during the small-pox epidemic of 1894 in the sweat-shops of Chicago has consisted in the enforcement of Sections 1 and 2 of the factories and workshops law, which are as follows:

SECTION 1. *Be it enacted by the People of the State of Illinois, represented in the General Assembly:* That no room or rooms, apartment or apartments, in any tenement or dwelling house used for eating or sleeping purposes, shall be used for the manufacture, in whole or in part, of coats, vests, trousers, knee-pants, overalls, cloaks, shirts, ladies' waists, purses, feathers, artificial flowers or cigars, except by the immediate members of the family living therein. Every such work-shop shall be kept in a cleanly state and shall be subject to the provisions of this act; and each of said articles made, altered, repaired or finished in any of such work-shops shall be subject to inspection and examination, as hereinafter provided, for the purpose of ascertaining whether said articles, or any of them, or any part thereof, are in a cleanly condition and free from vermin and any matter of an infectious and contagious nature; and every person so occupying or having control of any work-shop as aforesaid shall within fourteen days from the taking effect of this act, or from the time of beginning of work in any work-shop as aforesaid, notify the board of health of the location of such work-shop, the nature of the work there carried on, and the number of persons therein employed.

§ 2. If the board of health of any city or said State Inspector finds evidence of infectious or contagious diseases present in any work-shop or in goods manufactured or in process of manufacture therein, and if said board or inspector shall find said shop in an unhealty condition, the clothing and materials used therein to be unfit for use, said board or inspector shall issue such order or orders as the public health may require, and the board of health are hereby enjoined to condemn and destroy all such infectious and contagious articles.

As there are in Chicago between 950 and 1,000 licensed shops and about 25,000 other rooms in which garments are manufactured, it would be a hopeless task for any body of inspectors to attempt to enforce these provisions in all of them, and we can make no claim that this has been done. On the contrary the following record demonstrates the impossibility of guaranteeing safety for the purchasing public so long as tenement house manufacture is permitted.

When the presence of small-pox in the tenement house shops became apparent this office was already equipped with the latest lists of the wholesale houses, the contractors employed by them in so-called "outside" shops, the addresses of employes who work in the large garment factories by day, and carry home goods for work at night and on Sunday and, finally, with lists of the home finishers employed by the contractors.

The initial work embodied in our first annual report last December, had been carried steadily forward, and one inspector detailed exclusively to an uninterrupted search for evidence of infection in the shops in that district which has since been ravaged by small-pox.

On February 9 copies of the following circular were sent to each of the 176 wholesalers and merchant tailors who control the garment trades in Chicago, and to such contractors as had shops of any considerable size.

STATE OF ILLINOIS,
OFFICE OF FACTORY INSPECTOR,
247 W. POLK STREET,

CHICAGO, FEBRUARY 9, 1894.

The daily reports of inspectors filed in this office during the present month indicate renewed activity in the manufacture of clothing in Chicago, especially of cloaks, knee-pants and neckties. The workshops and dwellings in which this manufacture is carried on are found to be numerous in the districts in which small-pox cases have also been numerous.

Contractors working in these shops are reported obstinately negligent in regard to compliance with §§ 1 and 7 of the workshop law. Their failure to keep lists of the home finishers in their employ (§ 7) and the failure of the home finishers to notify the board of health of their addresses (§ 1) rendered it very difficult for inspectors of this office to find the finishers' work places and enforce that part of the law which provides for freedom from infection.

A rigid search of those districts in which clothing is manufactured has therefore been instituted, and will be maintained throughout the present clothing season.

All persons who work in a factory by day and carry away from it articles to be worked upon in their homes, and all persons who work some days in the week in a factory and some days at home for the same employer, come under § 1 of the law, and are required to comply with it by sending their names and addresses to the board of health.

Employers who permit articles to be taken from the factory or workshop to be worked upon at night or on Sunday, and returned to the factory, come under § 7 of the law, and are required to keep on file a complete list of the names and addresses of employés by whom such articles are taken.

. To save you possible loss of goods you are hereby notified that §§ 1 and 7 will be enforced by prosecuting all violations and by ordering infectious goods immediately destroyed, in accordance with §§ 9 and 2 of the law. Very truly yours,

FLORENCE KELLEY,
Factory Inspector.

Copies of this circular were also sent to the daily papers of Chicago, with a request for editorial notice pointing out the impending danger and urging obedience to the law.

Of the whole number of garment manufacturers in the city less than half a dozen took the trouble to obtain lists of the home finishers employed by their contractors, and, so far as known to the inspectors, no contractor voluntarily registered with the board of health, or required his home finishers to do so. So complete was the indifference of all concerned, both to the danger of infection and to our efforts to enforce these sections of the law, that in March we prosecuted, under § 1, Hyman Kapize, a cloakmaker living at 83 Wilson street, and working for F. Siegel & Bros., in their factory by day and in his tenement bed-room at night and on Sundays.

Tenement House Workers Violate the Law.

In the course of the trial Mr. Joseph Greenhut, statistician of the city board of health, who was summoned as a witness, testified that no contractor or home finisher had ever voluntarily complied either with the State law or with the city ordinance requiring registration, but that he was obliged to send out men from the board of health to compel the tailors to register under threat of prosecution and of having their shops closed as nuisances.

The prosecution and fining of Kapize produced no effect, although small-pox was already gaining a foothold among the sweater shops and home workers. It was manifestly hopeless to prosecute hundreds of the poorest of the poor—the home garment workers of the city—to compel them to register; and there was no prospect of any co-operation on the part of the wholesalers whose control over their outside employes is absolute. This control has been constantly shown throughout the epidemic, a hint from the down town foreman invariably finding instant compliance, when threats of arrest made by the inspectors were calmly defied. The problem, therefore, now was how to reach the comparatively few wholesalers and through them the multitude of tenement house workers.

A random search among a thousand shops and 25,000 to 30,000 other rooms being out of the question, we obtained from the city board of health a daily list of cases of infectious disease, compared these addresses with our office lists, and made immediate inspections of shops in and near the infected premises. In the course of these inspections we found so many cases of small-pox which had not been reported to us that we soon ceased to depend on the city hall lists alone, and supplemented them with the daily lists of diagnoses of the district physicians, of which the number varied, during a part of the time, from 30 to 47 in a single district in a day.

The Infected District.

In April it became clear that, while there was an occasional case of small-pox among the Swedish tailors on the north side, the disease was overwhelmingly epidemic in the Polish and Bohemian district extending from 16th street south to the river, and from May street westward to the city limits. Here we have found 273 different tenement houses infected, and the disease is still prevalent in this district.

The prejudice against vaccination, which is obstinate and widespread among the population in this part of the city, contributed largely to the spread of small-pox; and it was not until the tailors found their shops empty during the months which usually constitute the height of the season, that they reluctantly consented to vaccination for themselves and their employés. This change was brought about only when the press had published a mass of information, obtained from this office, of a nature so appalling that Dr. Arthur Reynolds, Commissioner of Health of Chicago, in response to public clamor issued the following circular to the garment manufacturers and wholesalers of the city, on the 27th of April:

GENTLEMEN :—From information furnished by the State Factory Inspectors, 1 am convinced that the danger of small-pox contagion is very great in the tenement house shops of this city where clothing is being made up. Not only are the so-called "sweat-shops" in the infected regions, but the men, women and children employed in them all live in these regions, and are daily exposed to the disease. The inspectors' investigations have shown that not more than five per cent. of these employés have been vaccinated.

It becomes my duty to see that this sanitary precaution is taken, and your co-operation is invited because you have work done in these shops. I suggest that you decline to give out any more work to outside shops until your contractors furnish proof that all their employés in the shops and those who take work from them to be finished at home, have been vaccinated. No excuse can be taken for neglect of this simple precaution.

The detailed record of inspections which follows shows the defiance of the law on the part of the local health authorities, and of the garment manufacturers from the wholesalers down to the home finishers, until May 12, when Commissioner Reynolds reluctantly consented, under threat of immediate mandamus proceedings, to destroy one lot of clothing, found at 699 Alport street, in an unquestionably infectious condition. Up to this time he had refused to comply with that part of § 2 of the law which provides that the local board of health shall condemn and destroy infectious clothing.

Goods Condemned and Destroyed.

Four different lots of goods, belonging to four different firms, having been condemned and destroyed on the infected premises, the effect upon the manufacturers and the local authorities was decisive. The City Board of Health provided a public sterilizer, and from this time the removal of patients to the pesthouse and the fumigation of infected premises was somewhat expedited.

Ineffectual Measures Adopted.

A meeting of representatives of the boards of health of Michigan, Wisconsin, Illinois, Ohio and Indiana, with representatives of the garment manufacturers of Chicago, was held at the Grand Pacific hotel, in this city, on Thursday, May 10. At this meeting we pointed out the impossibility of guaranteeing as non-infectious garments made in the tenement houses, by reason of the vast number of rooms to be watched, the vital interests of the tenants in concealing the disease, and the reckless manner in which garment workers were moving their shops and homes.

We urged upon the representatives of the manufacturers and the health authorities the necessity of suspending tenement house manufacture during at least six months, and of transferring all work to suitable factories. This the manufacturers' representatives united in calling an impossibility for the immediate present. We then urged them at least to refrain from sending out goods to be made up in the infected district. This measure no one could deem impossible, since there are shops in other districts of the city where the disease was not epidemic. This very moderate precautionary measure also was rejected, and instead a proposition was agreed upon to institute "an efficient daily inspection of all shops and workrooms." In view of the fact that the 30,000 garment workrooms of Chicago would require, for "an efficient daily inspection," fifteen hundred (1,500) inspectors empowered to force an entry into any bedroom, kitchen, stable, or cellar, at any hour, this project could not, in the nature of things, prove effectual, and this we pointed out.

Limitations of the Law.

That the measures taken have not been effectual in stopping the sending out of infectious clothing, this report amply shows. After two months added experience, the inspectors can only repeat, with renewed emphasis, the warning that there is no safety for the purchasing public while tenement house manufacture is tolerated, and express their conviction, that half-way measures of inspection are extremely dangerous because they lull the purchasing public into a false sense of security.

It cannot be too much emphasized that the difficulties in the way of successful inspection of all tenement house shops are insuperable difficulties, by reason of the vast number of the shops, and the shifting about of the workers. They are here to-day and gone to-morrow. It has been the sole occupation of a faithful and skillful factory inspector for a year to obtain lists of addresses of garment workers, but these lists require daily revision to keep them even approximately correct.

From the foregoing facts and from the record of illustrative cases which follows, it is clear that the factories and workshops act, in its present crude and imperfect form, has afforded a certain degree of protection to the purchasing public. Although it is impossible that any regulation of tenement house manufacture should render it free from the danger of spreading infection, yet the power vested in the State Inspectors to search for evidence of infection, and to compel the local authorities to destroy infectious goods, has served to check, to some extent, the sending of garments to be made up in the infectious district. Indeed, one of the largest firms sent no more work there after the first batch of goods was burned, and, although there were more than two hundred shops running in the district during the week ending May 26, the reports of our inspections through the month of June show that a number of the too-slowly alarmed manufacturers have at last partially withdrawn their work from this district. Through June, while we found little diminution of the disease, we have found a great number of shops on infectious premises closed.

It has seemed needless to recount in detail the scores of cases in which small-pox was found next door to a sweater shop, and no work in the shop; or where the disease was two or three doors away from a shop; or where the sweater was found working, but the inspection was made to ascertain whether the employés had been vaccinated and where they lived, with a view to investigating whether there was infection in their homes. The inspections made for the purpose of obtaining the sweater's new lists of home finishers, that these homes might be searched for the disease, have also been omitted, as adding nothing essential to the bill of particulars herewith submitted.

RECORD OF ILLUSTRATIVE CASES.

April 24, 1894—Anton Horky, 665 Alport Street, custom tailor for M. Born & Co., 250 Market Street. Inspectors Bisno and Stevens.

This shop is on the second floor rear, entrance through Horky's kitchen. The inspectors found one man working on a fine custom coat, another coat in process of manufacture, and Horky gone down town to get more work. Before they left, he returned with two more coats for Born & Co., and stated that he had been working steadily during the last two weeks. Horky's shop and living rooms are in the rear upper floor of a frame tenement house, in which four families are living. In the rear, lower floor, lives James Olisar, in whose family there has been small-pox for three weeks, seven cases and one death. A yellow card was placed on the side of the house two weeks ago, after a baby died, but no quarantine is maintained. The four children of Horky and the sick children of the Olisar family play together, and the two families use the same vaults.

Inspector Stevens reported to Commissioner Reynolds the condition of these premises, and required of him the destruction of the goods in Horky's home shop, in accordance with § 2 of the Factory and Workshop act. Commissioner Reynolds replied that under no circumstances would he destroy goods, as fumigation only was necessary. He promised to have the goods at 665 Alport street fumigated on Wednesday, April 25. Owing to the absence of accessible records in the city health department we have never been able to ascertain if this was done.

April 25—Inspector Stevens notified M. Born & Co., that their goods, now in Horky's possession, must not be received until they had been disinfected, and that Horky could do no more work in his shop at 665 Alport street, until it was separated from his living rooms as required by § 1 of the Workshop law.

April 26—Inspectors Bisno and Hickey visited Horky's shop, found no work on the premises and served notice on him to separate shop from dwelling.

There followed a recurrence of small-pox at 665 Alport street, on May 12, in the Varbeck family. In connection with this case especial attention is asked for the record of cases by streets, with which this report closes, as showing how heavy is the probability of recurrence where small-pox has appeared in a tenement house, the interval even exceeding in some houses the eighteen days which have been assumed to constitute the normal limit of recurrence. It is impossible to induce people as sorely in need as the garment-workers of Chicago, to suspend work during three weeks merely because some fellow tenant in a crowded tenement house has a sick child. And he must be both a sanguine optimist and comfortably ignorant of the ways of the dwellers in tenements, who expects of them any such reasonable precaution as isolation of the patient. Indeed, the intimacy bred of overcrowding is increased in times of sickness, and neighbors help with the nursing, sit up with the dead, and attend the funeral, with dogged disregard of the infectious nature of the malady.

April 24, 1894.—Simon Marsalck, 756 Alport Street, coatmaker for Kuh, Nathan & Fischer, Franklin and Van Buren Streets. Inspectors Stevens and Bisno.

The inspectors found Marsalek not working. The shop, in which eight persons are ordinarily employed, is a most filthy room, reached only through a kitchen in the same condition, the shop not being separated from Marsalek's living rooms, which are on the first floor of a rear house, behind a three story tenement, overcrowded with people. In this front house there had been two small-pox patients in the week ending April 21, and on the 21st Marsalek had returned to Kuh, Nathan & Fischer thirty-six coats made for them in his shop during the week.

April 25—Inspector Stevens notified Kuh, Nathan & Fischer to give no more work to Marsalek until he complied with § 1 of the law, separating his shop from his living rooms. The inspector also told them of the danger of contagion to which the goods returned to them on April 21 had been subjected.

Mr. Kuh gave orders that no more work should be given to Marsalek.

This case illustrates the impossibility of guarding against infection in tenement house shops. The presence of small-pox at 756 Alport street was not made known until the day of this inspection, while the time for an effective inspection was the previous week. On April 21 both the small-pox and the thirty-six coats were on the premises. On April 24, when it was announced that small-pox was here, both the patient and the coats were gone.

May 18—Inspectors Jones and Bisno again visited 756 Alport street. There are new cases of small-pox in the rear part of the front house. Marsalek was not working, and they found no work on the premises.

April 27, 1894.—Thomas Stankovich, 2111 Purple Street, Tailor for Ullman & Co., 284 State Street. Inspectors Bisno and Moran.

The inspectors did not find Stankovich working. They found the family of three living in two rooms, and that the tailor had his machine and did his work in a bed-room. He told them that he had returned work to Ullman & Co., on the previous day. There is small-pox in the house with Stankovich, in the rear of the same floor on which he lives and works. The inspectors notified Ullman & Co., that the work returned to them on the previous day by Stankovich was probably infected, and should be disinfected. The city board of health was requested to disinfect the coat at Ullman's, and also Stankovich's rooms.

May 9—Inspector Stevens was informed by Ullman & Co., in reply to an inquiry, that the coat returned to them by Stankovich had been fumigated.

April 28, 1894.—James Honota, 20 Zion Place, coat-maker for Hirsch, Elson & Co., 160-162 Market street. Inspectors Bisno and Moran.

Found working six persons in a shop on the first floor of a rear house. There were small-pox cases in the front house on the same premises. Inspectors found that Honota was sorting bundles of goods in his kitchen and in other ways was not properly separating his shop from his dwelling.

Monday, April 30, Hirsch, Elson & Co., were notified not to give more work to Honota until the danger of contagion on his premises was over, and until his shop had been properly separated from his living rooms. Owing to the absence of accessible records in the city health department, we have never been able to ascertain whether the goods in Honota's shop on this date were fumigated.

On May 9, Hirsch, Elson & Co., sent a representative to this office to state that the premises at 20 Zion Place had been declared by the district physician free from infection, and requesting permission to send further work there to Honota.

On May 10, there was a recurrence of small-pox at this number, and Inspector Jones notified Hirsch, Elson & Co., of the same.

In the week May 14–19 inclusive, a boy from Honota's shop came four times to this shop, with a certificate from Dr. Brand, the district physician, stating that it was safe to work in this shop. Hirsch, Elson & Co., refused to give the work unless this certificate was endorsed by the State Factory Inspector, and this endorsement naturally could not be given for any shop in a locality so infected as Zion Place. The record of cases by streets shows that there were, on May 19, five cases in Zion Place, a street only one block long.

April 30, 1894.—J. Kolka, 625 W. 21st street, a coat-maker for Pfaelzer, Sutton & Co., Franklin and Van Buren streets. Inspectors Stevens and Bisno.

This shop is in the rear of Kolka's living rooms on the first floor. The entrance is by a side door used also in going to the living rooms. The inspectors found Kolka and his wife, with two men visitors, in the shop, and sixteen coats for Pfaelzer, Sutton & Co., in process of manufacture. The living rooms of the Kolka family were closed, and in process of fumigation. A ten-year old son of Kolka died of small-pox on Saturday, April 29. The fumigator from the board of health had left the premises before the State inspectors reached it, but he had not fumigated the shop nor disinfected these coats, telling the Kolkas that it was not necessary, although the parents of the child had tended their patient and worked on the coats at the same time. The inspectors asked Kolka when he returned the last work to the firm employing him. Kolka does not talk easily in English, and Mrs. Kolka, who attends to that part of the business, positively asserts that it was several weeks since they had any work except the sixteen coats then on the premises, and that none had been returned since the boy was taken sick.

Inspector Stevens reported to Pfaelzer, Sutton & Co. the infectious condition of the sixteen coats on Kolka's premises, and received their promise not to accept the goods until said goods had been properly disinfected. The inspector repeated to them Mrs. Kolka's assurance that no goods had been returned to them since April 13, and requested them to ascertain from their books if this was correct. The books showed that Mrs. Kolka had returned to them sixty-one coats on April 23, while small-pox was in the house. They were enabled to identify the coats by their ticket system, and as these coats were in a separate lot they requested that these also might be disinfected and agreed to keep them boxed away from other goods until this was done.

14

Inspector Stevens went from Pfaelzer, Sutton & Co.'s store to the board of health, and finding Commissioner Reynolds absent, reported this case in detail to Secretary McCarthy of the board, receiving his assurance that both lots of goods should be disinfected the next morning.

May 5—Mr. Meyer, from Pfaelzer, Sutton & Co., after waiting five days for the city board of health, reported to this office that no one from the board of health had yet visited their place, that the sixty-one coats were not yet disinfected, that the sixteen coats had been returned from Kolka's without the knowledge of the firm, and that they feared that these also were not disinfected. At her request, Mr. Meyer accompanied Inspector Stevens to Commissioner Reynold's office to inquire why the disinfection had not been done as promised by Secretary McCarthy. Neither Commissioner Reynolds nor his secretary had any excuse to offer. They did not know why no fumigator had been to the business place of Pfaelzer, Sutton & Co., and had no records to consult, to determine whether the shop and coats at 625 W. 21st street had been fumigated. The inspector finally succeeded in getting a reluctant promise from Secretary McCarthy that the two lots of coats at Pfaelzer, Sutton & Co.'s should be fumigated this (Saturday) afternoon, or Monday morning. In the presence of the inspector Secretary McCarthy tried to dissuade Mr. Meyer from having this done, because of the trouble involved.

May 7—Inspector Stevens visited Pfaelzer, Sutton & Co., in the afternoon, and found that the city fumigator had not yet been there; then visited Secretary McCarthy, and gave him until 9 o'clock the next morning to fulfill his promise.

May 8—At 10 o'clock a message was received at this office from Pfaelzer, Sutton & Co. that the fumigator was there.

The utter inadequacy of the measures taken to prevent the spread of infection in these seventy-seven coats is apparent. The Kolka boy was sick a week before a doctor was called, when the child was dying. Before the report of the diagnosis reached the city board of health or this office the child was dead and buried. It was nine days after this before the city board of health fumigated the coats, and fumigation, under these circumstances, can by no means be considered a guarantee of disinfection. These goods should have been burned; but the commissioner of health refused to comply with § 2 of the Workshop Act, which enjoins the board of health to condemn and destroy goods under such circumstances. .

April 30, 1894.—John Zika, 269 W. 20th street, custom tailor for M. Born & Co., 256 Market street; I. Kreha and J. Freund, contractors for. Kohn Bros., Market and Monroe streets. Inspectors Stevens and Bisno.

On this date small-pox cases at 269 W. 20th street appeared upon the records of the city board of health. The records of this office showed three tailors living and working on the same premises, namely: John Zika, working for M. Born & Co., and I. Kreha and J. Freund, contractors for Kohn Bros. The inspectors found two frame houses on the lot, with small-pox signs on both. In the rear house they conversed with a patient in an advanced stage of the disease (there being no attempt at quarantine) and learned from his wife that all three tailors had moved out, two of them after the small-pox signs were on the houses. The small-pox patient in the front house died on Saturday night, two days previous to this inspection, and all the tenants then moved away. While the inspectors were investigating in the rear house, the small-pox sign was taken from the front house, and the "To Rent" sign put up.

The inspectors continued their search for the three tailors, and located Zika at 722 S. Morgan street, where they found him at work with nine employés. He told the inspectors that he had moved his shop and his family from 269 W. 20th street the Saturday night before, on the day of the death of the patient in the front house. The inspectors found work on hand, thirteen fine custom coats for M. Born & Co., and took the numbers of six of these coats which had been brought from Born's by Zika on April 27 and 28, and consequently had been in the infected house.

Inspector Stevens reported all these circumstances in detail to Mr. Kirschbarger, of the firm of M. Born & Co., warning them not to receive any work from Zika until it had been disinfected, and not to give him any more work until time had elapsed sufficient to determine whether or not Zika, his family, or his help, had contracted small-pox at 269 W. 20th street.

The same afternoon (April 30) Inspector Stevens reported all these facts to Commissioner Reynolds, and urged him to have steps taken immediately to prevent the spread of contagion already probable in consequence of the failure to quarantine 269 W. 20th street, asking that, since he refused to destroy goods, he would at least be very careful to have the infected garments which had been removed to 722 S. Morgan street thoroughly fumigated.

May 9—Inspector Stevens called on Commissioner Reynolds, but neither he nor Secretary McCarthy could tell whether anything had been done with these goods. Commissioner Reynolds referred the inspector to Dr. Brand, physician in charge of the small-pox epidemic in the district in which these cases were, as the proper person to give the desired information.

May 10—Inspectors Stevens and Bisno repeated to Dr. Brand the questions asked of Commissioner Reynolds the day before. Dr. Brand could not give them any information, as his fumigators report to him verbally, and he had no office records.

May 1—Inspector Stevens notified Kohn Bros. of the small-pox cases at 269 W. 20th street, and asked their assistance in locating Kreha and Freund, the two tailors in their employ who had been living and working at this number. Their list showed that Kreha had returned some overcoats to them the day before, but had not notified them that he had moved, nor had he told them of the infection at 269 W. 20th street.

May 2—A letter was received from Kohn Bros. stating that I. Kreha had removed from 269 W. 20th street some time before, and was now located at 415 W. 17th street. Freund had not been in their employ for some months, and we have not since been able to locate him.

The disappearance of Freund is an illustration of the weakness of those clauses of the law which require the manufacturers to keep correct lists of the outside shops in their employ and garment-workers to register their home shops with the board of health. His name was not filed with the board of health as moving from 269 W. 20th street. He may have carried away from the infected house to another tenement house any quantity of goods belonging to some firm other than Kohn Bros.

In the case of these three tailors, as in the Kolka case, the arrival of the factory inspectors on the infected premises, while it followed immediately upon their learning that infection was there, was yet too late to prevent the sending out of infectious goods as contemplated by the Workshop law. Before the city board of health was aware that small-pox was at 269 W. 20th street, the disease had made a week's inroad among the tenants crowded in the two houses, and in that time garments had been manufactured on the premises, returned to the merchant tailors, and thence, without doubt, had gone to the customers on whose orders the garments had been made. After the district physician had diagnosed the sickness here as small-pox, the failure of the city authorities to quarantine the place made it possible for the tailors to scatter and for Zika to move his infectious goods to another tenement house. Nor have we any assurance that, after we had, as a result of our inspection, notified both the manufacturers and the city board of health that these goods had been exposed to infection, anything was done to the goods to remove the danger.

This feeble result from our utmost efforts under the provisions of the Workshop act, compelled the step of warning the purchasing public through the daily papers. The Kolka and Zika cases with other substantiated information concerning infected clothing made in this district, were made public. The threat of quarantine of Chicago garments by the boards of health of the surrounding states, and the meeting in this city of the state boards, followed.

April 30, 1894—Joseph Dvorak, 745 W. 18th street, pants-maker for Strauss, Yondorf & Rose, Market and Quincy streets. Inspector Bisno.

Dvorak was found with three people at work in his dwelling rooms, which are in the rear house. There is small-pox in the front house on these premises. Strauss, Yondorf & Rose were notified to give no more work to Dvorak until he had a shop in accordance with § 1 of the law, and were also warned that their goods now on his premises were exposed to contagion. Owing to the absence of accessible records of the city board of health it is impossible to learn whether the goods in this shop were disinfected.

May 1, 1894—Emma Gardner, 305 W. Polk street, pants-maker for C. P. Kellogg & Co., 167 Franklin street. Inspectors Stevens and Bisno.

Mrs. Gardner's shop is in her kitchen, first floor rear, where the inspectors found her working with her husband on twenty-five pairs of pants for C. P. Kellogg & Co. There had been a small-pox patient in the house during the last five days, who was removed to the pest-house last evening.

C. P. Kellogg & Co. were notified of the danger to which their goods had been exposed, and advised that the same be removed and disinfected. Disinfection followed by Board of Health.

May 2, 1894—James Prepeschal, 31 Zion Place, coat-moker for Ullman, Guthman & Silverman, Franklin and Monroe streets. Inspector Bisno.

Found employing ten persons in building on rear of lot, facing alley, small-pox next door, at No. 35 Zion Place, there being no No. 33. On May 18 there was a recurrence of the disease at No. 35, four cases. Owing to the absence of accessible records of the city board of health it is impossible to learn whether the goods in this shop were disinfected.

May 2, 1894—Joseph Belinsky, 723 W. 18th street, cloak-maker for Joseph Beifeld & Co., 253 Jackson street. Inspector Bisno.

This shop is on the first floor, with an entrance on the side street. Belinsky was found not working. There is small-pox in the same house, upstairs.

May 2, 1894—Charles G. Hirst & Brother, 144 Vedder street, pants-makers for Hirsch, Elson & Co., 160-162 Market street; Cahn, Wampold & Co., 204-210 Monroe street; Ullman, Guthman & Silverman, 229 Monroe street; E. Rothschild & Bro., 203-205 Monroe street, Work Brothers, corner Market and VanBuren streets; Einstein & Co., 226 Franklin street. Inspector Bisno.

The inspector found twenty-seven persons working in this shop. There is small-pox next door.

May 2, 1894—Herman Carlson, or Wahlstrom & Carlson, 144 Vedder street, vest-makers for D'Ancona and Continental Tailoring Co. Inspector Bisno.

The inspector found fourteen persons working in this shop. There is small-pox next door.
—2 S.

18

May 2, 1894—Dahlborn & Odell, 144 Vedder street, vest-makers for M. Born & Co., 250 Market street. Inspector Bisno.

The inspector found seventeen persons working in this shop. There is small-pox next door.

May 2, 1894—Frank A. Lindholm, 144 Vedder street, vest-maker for Nicoll the Tailor, Clark and Adams street, and for the American Tailors, Clark and Monroe streets. Inspector Bisno.

The inspector found twenty-three persons working in this shop. There is small-pox next door.

May 2, 1894—F. E. Hallberg, 144 Vedder street, pants-maker for Kohn Brothers, Monroe street and Market. Inspector Bisno.

The inspector found sixteen persons working in this shop. There is small-pox next door.

The preceding five cases call attention to the fact that there are in Chicago a few buildings occupied exclusively by sweaters that are distinct and separate from any tenement houses. The very great advantage of these over the tenement house shops, to the sweater and his employés as well as to the manufacturer and the purchasing public, is shown in the case of these five shops. The building in which they are located is used for factory purposes only. It is a brick building, four stories and basement, well-lighted, in good sanitary condition, with steam power supplied in all the shops.

When the inspector visited these shops on May 2, there being small-pox next door, he met and conferred with the physician in charge of small-pox in that district, from whom he learned that all the employés in the five shops had been successfully vaccinated and that the goods in process of manufacture might, therefore, be regarded as non-infectious. Had the shops been in a tenement house, with families commingling and children playing together, the decision must have been very different.

May 5, 1894—Emanuel Bubnek, 426 W. 17th street, custom coat-maker. Inspector Bisno.

This inspector found this man, with one assistant, working with one coat in process of manufacture and one in a bundle on which work had not been begun. There had been small-pox in the house for some days, on the same floor with the tailor, in a room in the rear of his shop and living room. A boy nineteen years old died there of the disease the previous night (May 4). The yellow card was on the house, but there was no quarantine. The inspector asked Bubnek for whom he worked but he refused to answer. After much urging, he said that he worked for Born on Market street. Inspector Bisno warned him not to remove the coats until they had been disinfected, and reported the case at this office.

Inspector Stevens notified M. Born & Co., and was informed
by Mr. Kirchbarger of the firm that no such man was in their
employ. At her request he had their lists of outside contractors carefully examined, and still found that they had no tailor
named Bubnek, nor any tailor living at 426 W. 17th street.

May 6—Inspector Bisno went again to Bubnek's house and
shop. Bubnek and his assistant were still working on one of
the coats, and the other had disappeared. The workman employed by Bubnek insisted that the coat they were working on
belonged to him. Both tailors then took refuge in the Bohemian
tongue, claiming that they could not understand English, and
when the inspector brought in an interpreter no further satisfac-
tion was obtained, no information as to the missing coat and
nothing as to the employer of the men. The coat in hand was
of a quality and style which indicated that it was not to be
worn by any workingman.

This case illustrates one of the disastrously weak spots of the
law as it stands, the failure to provide a penalty for disregard
of orders issued by the inspectors in regard to infectious shops
under § 2. Very rarely has the sweater obeyed the order to
hold goods for disinfection. The procedure is as follows: An
inspector finding small-pox in the sweater's family and the man
at work upon an expensive custom made coat instructs him to
hold it for disinfection. The inspector then goes to the nearest
telephone and notifies the merchant tailor that the coat must
be sterilized and if not sterilized will be destroyed. Before the
sterilizer's wagon can reach the sweater's dwelling the coat is on
its way to the merchant tailor's store. If the merchant is afraid
of small-pox the sweater is warned off the premises. If, however,
the merchant tailor rises superior to the fear of epidemic and
the unsuspecting customer is in a hurry for his coat, or if, as
is often the case, the suit is destined for a customer in some
other city, it is promptly delivered, and the law provides no
penalty for either the sweater or the merchant.

Section 2 of the work-shop act empowers inspectors to issue
such orders "as the public health may require," but provides
no penalty for the failure to comply with the orders. The law
should be amended by the insertion in the penalty clause § 8 of
the following words, "or any order issued in writing by the inspectors under the provisions of this act," making this clause
of the section read:

"Any person, firm or corporation who fails to comply with
any provisions of this act, *or any order issued in writing by the
inspectors under the provisions of this act*, shall be deemed guilty
of a misdemeanor and on conviction thereof shall be fined not
less than three dollars nor more than one hundred dollars for
each offense."

May 7, 1894.—James Doubek, 796 W. 17th street, pants and coat-maker for C. P. Kellogg & Co., 167 Franklin street; and for C. & L. Nye, 231 Blue Island avenue. Inspectors Stevens and Bisno.

Doubek's shop is on the first floor, rear, of a frame tenement house. He lives on the premises, upstairs, and has two children. The family living on the first floor front also has children, and uses the same hall and outbuildings as the Doubek family, and, in fact, the two families are practically one so far as associating together goes. During the week preceding May 7 there was small-pox on the first floor, in the room next to Doubek's shop. A boy was taken from this room to the pest-house on Saturday, May 5. All through this week of infection Doubek was working. He told the inspectors that the work was done for Kellogg and for Nye. He had on hand at the time of this inspection eighteen pairs of pants.

Inspector Stevens ascertained that Doubek had no work for C. P. Kellogg & Co., and warned them of the danger of recurrence of disease, so that no work should be sent to this shop until it was known whether the failure to quarantine resulted in more cases.

Inspector Bisno notified the Nye firm to the same effect, and as the pants in Doubek's shop belonged to this firm, they were warned not to receive the garments until the same had been disinfected. Disinfection of the goods was then ordered. Owing to the absence of accessible records in the health department we have not been able to learn whether this was done.

Eight days later there were cases of small-pox at 797 W. 17th street, and again cases on June 8, when the disease was also in other houses in that block. At this time Doubek's shop was visited by Inspectors Kelley and Bisno, and he was not found working.

May 9, 1894—James Chesek, 901 W. 19th street, coat-maker for M. Born & Co., 256 Market street. Inspector Bisno.

This is a frame tenement house, one of the tenants being the contrator Chesek, who has a shop in the rear, ground floor. He was found working on coats for M. Born & Co., with twelve persons employed. There is small-pox next door, at 897 W. 19th street (there is no 899), the yellow card is on the door, and the place is supposed to be quarantined. Inspector Bisno saw a little girl coming from the upper floor at 897 eating a banana, and saw her enter the shop of Chesek. He questioned the child, who said that she was Chesek's cousin, and was living with him now, that the sick people were her brothers and sisters, and that she had been up to see them and carry them some bananas. The inspector then reported these details at this office, the relations of the infected family to the shop were further investigated and the child's statement substantiated.

May 9—M. Born & Co. were notified that their goods at 901 W. 19th street were believed to be in an infectious condition. An order on Commissioner Reynolds to condemn and destroy the goods in accordance with § 2 of the Workshop Law was sent to the office of the board of health by a district messenger boy, and was receipted for by Secretary McCarthy of the board.

May 10—At 1 P. M. Inspector Bisno visited Chesek's shop, found the goods still there, and the full force of employés at work.

May 11—Inspectors Kelley and Stevens called on Commissioner Reynolds at his office, at 11 A. M., to ascertain why no action had been taken by the board of health on this case. Commissioner Reynolds said that he had lost the order which he had received to destroy these goods. Inspector Kelley immediately served another order upon the Commissioner to destroy the goods, and informed him that Inspector Bisno was now on guard at this shop, and requested that an agent of the board of health be sent to destroy the goods. While this conversation was going on in the office of the board of health, Inspector Bisno had gone to the shop of Chesek, and found that the goods had already been taken away. He was informed that they had been returned to Born & Co.

In this case, as in the Bubnek case, the failure to hold the goods as the inspector ordered, shows the weakness of § 8 of the Workshop Act. For want of a penalty for this offense, it was found impossible to make a warning example by prosecution of either Chesek or M. Born & Co.

May 9, 1894.—Frank Jirsa, 444 W. 19th street, coat-maker for Simon, Leopold & Solomon, 165-167 Market street. Inspector Bisno.

Jirsa was found working in the basement of this tenement house, making coats. There is small-pox next door, at 446 W. 19th street.

May 19—Inspectors Kelley and Stevens visited this shop, which is a low, dark room, with a window opening upon the yard and an entrance through a dirty kitchen, Jirsa, with his family of four persons, having only one other room, a small bed-room. Jirsa employs no outside help, his little girl, fourteen years old, working with him. There was still small-pox at 446 W. 19th street. Simon, Leopold & Solomon were notified of the unsanitary condition of Jirsa's shop, and of the disease next door.

This case illustrates the inadequacy of § 1 of the law, which permits the manufacture of garments in kitchens or bed-rooms, provided no persons outside the members of the family are there employed. The danger of the spread of contagion in Jirsa's work in his living room is precisely the same as though he had a shop separate from his living rooms on the premises.

May 9, 1894.—Joseph Mydlil, 444 W. 19th street, coat-maker for Hart, Schaffner & Marx, Jackson and Market streets. Inspector Bisno.

This shop is in a house on the rear of the lot, with windows on the yard and alley; the contractor lives over the shop. He was found working, with twelve persons employed. There is small-pox next door, at 446 W. 19th street.

May 16—Inspectors Kelley and Stevens visited this shop, and found eleven persons working; four of these live in the tenement house, 444 W. 19th street, and one at 446 W. 19th street, where there have been cases of small-pox during eight days; the eleven employés all live in the infected district, with small-pox all about them. Hart, Schaffner & Marx were notified of the danger of contagion in this shop, and that it might be necessary, at any time, to order the infected goods there condemned and destroyed, in accordance with § 2 of the Workshop law. Mr. Hart promised that all goods then in the shop should be immediately sterilized, and that no more goods should be sent to it while the danger of infection lasted.

In the Mydlil and Jirsa cases is shown the danger of spread of the contagion wherever garment manufacture is carried on in tenement houses. With continuous cases of small-pox next door, with employes living on infected premises, it was yet impossible for the inspectors to prove that goods in these two shops were actually infected. There only remained a warning to the manufacturers, with a statement of the facts showing the probability of infection. If the manufacturers continued to send goods to the shops, the inspectors could do nothing except continue to watch them. The result in this case is shown in a subsequent record, June 6. Anton Benesek.

May 10, 1894—J. Frick, 929 Hinman street, contractor for L. Loewenstein & Co., 122 Franklin street. Inspectors Bisno and Stevens.

This is a basement shop, and was found without any work in it. Across a narrow hall, in the same basement, there had been a small-pox patient removed to the pest-house on the day of this inspection. Loewenstein & Co. were notified of the danger of infection of this shop, and requested not to send work there at present.

May 24—Inspectors Kelley and Stevens found Frick's shop occupied by two girls who had formerly been employed by him there, and who are living and working in the shop now, eating and sleeping there, and making denim jackets for a firm at 46 Canalport avenue. The inspectors found that the girls had been vaccinated, and as there had been no recurrence of small-pox in this tenement house, they were permitted to remain.

May 2, 1894—Peter Zitnek, 699 Alport street, coat-maker for E. Rothschild & Bro., 205 Monroe street. Inspector Bisno.

Zitnek was found working with four employes, on the first floor rear of a tenement house, his family living on the same floor. He had on hand forty-three coats in process of manufacture, belonging to Rothschild & Bros. The inspector notified the firm that these coats were in an infectious condition, as there is small-pox in the same house, on the same floor, and the children of the family in which the sickness is were found at play with the children of Zitnek. The case was also reported to the physician in charge of this district, with a request that these coats be promptly fumigated and removed from the infected premises.

May 10—Inspector Bisno found the same forty-three coats still in Zitnek's shop. Inspector Stevens then went to the headquarters of Dr. Brand, the responsible physician of the board of health for this district, and endeavored to learn if these goods had been fumigated or in any way disinfected. Neither Dr. Brand nor his assistant, Dr. Hunt, could give any information. They said that they had no records which could be consulted to show whether the goods had been fumigated. The house at 699 Alport street was still nominally in quarantine, the yellow card on the door, and the probability of infection in these goods had become a certainty, as the families had not been at all separated since May 2, any more than before that date. The record of cases by streets shows the following: small-pox in Vonchura family, May 1, 4 cases; Henic family, May 3; Hossman family, May 11; all tenants at 699 Alport street. the house in which Zitnek lived and worked and in which were the forty-three coats ordered fumigated and taken away on May 2.

May 11—An order was issued for Commissioner Reynolds to destroy these goods in accordance with § 2 of the law. An inspector was sent out by him from the department of health, to these premises, who reported to him—on an entirely different premises—that he could find neither small-pox nor goods.

May 12—Inspector Bisno again visited the shop of Zitner, at 699 Alport street, and found the goods still there, and that nothing had been done to them. Upon receiving this report, Inspector Kelley again served written notice on Commissioner Reynolds to destroy these goods in accordance with § 2 of the Workshop law, and notified him that if these goods were not destroyed by 2 p. m. of the same day a petitition in mandamus proceedings would be filed before the court closed. Before 2 p. m. of this day the forty-three coats were burned in the presence of Inspector Bisno by agents of the department of health.

May 11, 1894—A. Vaneschek, 663 Alport street, coat-maker for Hirsch, Elson & Co., 160-162 Market street. Inspector Bisno.

In this shop there were found eighty-three coats, with two men working. It is a home shop, not properly separated from living rooms, and the children of the tailor were in the shop. They were also playing with other children who belonged to families where there is small-pox, the disease being at 665 and at 667 Alport street, as well as in other houses in the vicinity.

A communication was sent to Vanescheck's employers of which the following is a copy:

May 12, 1894.

Messrs. Hirsch, Elson & Co., 160-162 Market Street, Chicago:

GENTLEMEN:—An inspector from this office has found garments belonging to your firm at 663 Alport street, with small-pox next door, and the children of the infected house playing with the children of the tailor in whose shop your goods now are. As this may technically not be sufficient evidence of infection present in this shop to warrant us in ordering the goods destroyed without your consent, you are hereby notified that there is small-pox at 665 and 667 Alport street, and that there is no isolation possible for your goods in such closely packed tenement house shops and dwellings. We therefore asked your written consent to the destruction of all goods found on these premises to-day.

Yours very truly,

FLORENCE KELLEY.

At the request of Mr. Hirsch the goods in Vaneschek's shop were held until the steam sterilizer had been provided by the city, after which the goods were sterilized before they were received by Hirsch, Elson & Co.

May 11, 1894.—James Dvorak, 663 Alport street. Inspector B sno.

Dvorak's shop is in the basement of this tenement house, where he was found working alone, with several pairs of pants in process of manufacture. His name does not appear on any of the lists of outside contractors furnished by the manufacturers to this office, and he refused to tell the inspector for whom he was working. He was instructed not to deliver the goods but to hold them for disinfection. He moved out taking his goods with him, before any further action could be taken, and has not since been located.

May 12, 1894.—David Schwartz, 704 W. 18th street, cloak-maker for F. Siegel & Bro., 222-228 Market street. Inspectors Kelley and Bisno.

This shop is in the basement of the rear house on the lot with windows opening on the alley. On this date seven persons were employed in the shop. The inspectors found the yellow card posted on a door inside the front house. They immediately made an inventory of the goods in the shop, finding one hundred and twenty-five cloaks for children in process of manufacture and in bundles, and two of the persons in the shop unvaccinated. The shop was then ordered closed. The inspectors, learning that there were ten families, sixty-five persons, living on this lot, proceeded to examine the arms of the persons then on the premises, forty in all. Of these forty persons they found eighteen vaccinated. In one family they found four children in different stages of the disease. One flat was locked and darkened and access to it could not be gained. Subsequently it was ascertained that there was small-pox there also. As an illustration of the total absence of quarantine, it may be mentioned that while this inspection of arms was going on, a milkman came through the houses serving milk to the ten families, and two children came home from their day's work in a candy factory, to which they had gone from rooms adjoining those occupied by the four sick children.

Inspector Kelley telephoned Commissioner Reynolds of the four cases of small-pox at this number in addition to the case indicated by the yellow card, and asked that an immediate official diagnosis be made of the cases, and the tenents all vaccinated.

Monday, May 14, Inspectors Kelley and Bisno again visited the premises, 704 W. 18th street, and found everything exactly as before,.except that the yellow card had been removed to the outside door. The following notification was then sent:

May 14, 1894.

Messrs. F. Siegel & Bros., 222-228 Market Street.

GENTLEMEN:—There are at 704 W. 18th street one hundred and twenty-five cloaks belonging to your firm. As there has been small-pox at this number for several days past, we have notified the tailor in whose possession the cloaks are, David Schwartz, not to remove them until so ordered by us. He was also notified to discontinue work on these premises. If the city should provide a sterilizer within forty-eight hours, as I am informed that it is perfectly possible to do, and if these goods are kept quarantined in a manner satisfactory to us, it may be possible to sterilize them and render them fit for removal. The shop must, of course, be kept sealed. Assuming that you will hold your tailor strictly to these conditions, I beg to remain, yours respectfully,

FLORENCE KELLEY.

May 17—The terms proposed in this letter having been observed. and the sterilizer being now ready, the one hundred and twenty-five cloaks were removed in the presence of Inspector Hickey. They were taken from the windows of the shop directly into the alley, the inspector not permitting them to be carried to the front by the narrow entrance, as there were now six cases of small-pox on the premises and five other patients had been removed to the pest house on the previous day.

Could there be a more appalling example of the possibilities of tenement house manufacture than this case shows, with sixty-five people living on the premises, of whom but eighteen were vaccinated, eleven cases of small-pox among them in a single week, and men and women coming from tenement houses in all directions to manufacture woolen garments for children while the first five small-pox cases were running their course?

May 12, 1894.—F. Parlac, 909 W. 17th street, coat-maker for Cahn, Wampold & Co., 204-210 Monroe street. Inspectors Kelley and Bisno.

Parlac lives and works in rear rooms on the ground floor of a frame tenement house. In the ground floor lives one Dolezal, whose child died there of small-pox on Thursday, May 10, and was not buried until Saturday, May 12, the day of this inspection, after an illness lasting from Sunday, May 6. The inspectors found the yellow card on Dolezal's door, and in Parlac's shop, three fathers, three mothers, and six children living on these premises; three adult visitors, and three children from neighboring houses. An examination of the arms of all these people showed but three vaccinated. The tailor, Parlac, asked Inspector Kelley where he could be vaccinated, alleging that Dr. Brand had given him permission to bring goods to his shop as soon as he was vaccinated.

Parlac's employers were notified of the danger of infection in his shop as follows:

May 15, 1894.

Messrs. Cahn, Wampold & Co., 204-210 Monroe St.:

GENTLEMEN:—You have a contractor named Parlac, having his shop in his living rooms, at 909 W. 17th street. There was a child sick with small-pox in the same house last week, which died on Thursday last, and the sickness was not recognized as small-pox until the child was dead. The house was not quarantined, and it was not fumigated until Monday of this week. Consequently the disease has spread through all the neighborhood, and one case is to-day at the next door, 907 W. 17th street.

None of your goods are on Parlac's premises to-day at 4 P. M. and we send you this warning in order that you may refrain from giving him any work until the danger of contagion has passed.

Yours truly,

FLORENCE KELLEY.

May 16—Inspector Kelley again visited 909 W. 17th street, and found Parlac at work in his shop on goods for this firm. At this time the yellow card was still on the adjoining house, 907 W. 17th street.

May 14, 1894—Wm. Farber, 858 W. 20th street, pants-maker for L. C. Wachsmuth & Co., 122 Market street. Inspector Kelley.

While at the tailor shop of F. Parlac 909 W. 17th street, on this date, Inspector Kelley observed the yellow card next door, at 907, and on examination found that the patient, Herman Kramp, had been taken sick on Thursday, May 10, the day of the death from small-pox on Parlac's premises, but had not been recognized as a small-pox case until Friday. On this Thursday and Friday, May 10 and 11, his sister Bertha Kramp worked in the coat shop of Wm. Farber. She worked in the shop on Saturday also, and the only reason that she refrained from her usual avocation on this Monday of the inspection was that the day was a church holiday.

Farber's shop is in the basement of a tenement house with sixteen persons employed. Farber was notified to hold his goods for disinfection, and not to employ the girl, Bertha Kramp, again until further notice.

May 15—The firm of L. C. Wachsmuth & Co. was notified not to receive the goods from Farber's shop until they had been sterilized. Farber was given time to complete his work, and the sterilization was ordered on May 19.

In connection with the Farber case, we call attention to another danger from tenement house manufacture. In very many instances in this infected district during the last three months we have found on file in the shop a certificate issued by a district physician, stating that the shop was in a good sanitary condition. and giving permission for manufacture to be carried on therein. Such a certificate was shown by Wm. Farber. We should fail in our duty to the State and the purchasing public if we did not record our opinion, based upon our experience in this epidemic, that no certificate of this nature can be safely given by any physician who does not visit the homes of all the employés of the shop, and keep such homes under his daily inspection as long as the certificate is in force. That concealed cases were everywhere in the infected district during these months is known to all who watched the course of the epidemic, and the fact that, even where cases were known, quarantine was not maintained is equally a matter of general knowledge. That physicians made a practice, under such circumstances, of certifying that shops were free from contagion when they did not know where the workers of the shop lived, or the condition of their homes, is one more argument against all tenement house manufacture.

May 13, 1894—John Cerenak, 645 Throop street. coat-maker for A. A. Devore & Sons, Michigan Avenue, corner Adams street. Inspector Bisno.

The inspector found in Cerenak's shop, which is one of his living rooms, in this tenement house, a coat for the Devore firm in process of manufacture on Sunday, May 13. A boy lay dead of small-pox on the same premises, after several days illness. The man declined to name any other owner for the coat than himself, and was notified by the inspector not to remove it until it had been fumigated.

May 14—The firm of A A. Devore & Co. were notified from this office of the facts in the Cerenak case, and replied by letter that the coat belonged to them, and that they would rather it should be destroyed than returned to them.

May 15—An order was served on Commissioner Reynolds to condemn and destroy this coat in accordance with § 2 of the Workshop law. Dr. Henry Reynolds accompanied Inspector Bisno to the premises, and demanded the coat from Cerenak, showing him the letter from Cerenak's employers, A. A. Devore

& Co., asking for its destruction. Cerenak refused to give up the coat unless paid $16 for it, and for making another one which had been returned to the firm previously. Dr. Henry Reynolds then went away, saying to Inspector Bisno that he would return for the coat the next day, bringing police to take it, if necessary. Some days later he informed Inspector Bisno that he did not go back for this coat, and did not know what, if anything, had been done with it. It was then too late for inspectors from this office to trace the coat, which had disappeared.

May 14, 1894—John Feuhoff, 2949 Emerald avenue, coat-maker for Kauffman & Bro., 180 Adams street. Inspector Bisno.

This shop is in the basement of a rear frame tenement house, both houses being full of people. There are six persons employed, of whom four live on the premises. There is small-pox at 2951, and no quarantine is maintained. The yellow card has been kept, throughout the illness, posted on a rear door where it could be seen only from the rear of the lot.

Kauffman & Bro. were notified of the danger of infection to their goods in Feuhoff's shop, and advised to send no more work there until the danger is over.

May 14, 1894—F. J. Dolezal, 856 S. Wood street, coat-maker for Loewenstein & Co., 122 Franklin street. Inspectors Jones and Bisno.

This shop is on the first floor rear, and there is small-pox on the second floor front. Dolezal was found without work in his shop. One patient died of the disease last night, and another is sick in the house, and there is no quarantine. Loewenstein & Co. were notified of the infectious condition of these premises, and advised to send no more work to this shop until danger of contagion is passed.

May 15, 1894—John Bozovsky. 705 W. 16th street, coat-maker for Kuppenheimer & Co., Monroe and Franklin streets. Inspector Bisno.

This shop is in a frame dwelling house, and is not separated from Bozovsky's living rooms; there are nine persons employed and the inspector found that they had not been vaccinated. They all live in the infected district, and there is small-pox in the vicinity of the shop. Kuppenheimer & Co. were notified of these facts, and warned of the danger of giving work out for this shop under these conditions. The employés were immediately vaccinated by order of the firm.

May 14, 1894.—John Smethoma, 1189 Albany avenue, contractor for A. L. Singer & Co., 168-170 Market street. Inspector Kelley.

Dr. Brand telephoned that he had found bundles of goods for manufacture on the premises of John Smethoma, 1189 Albany avenue, which he believed to be infectious, for the following reasons: An undertaker, now living at 1117 Albany avenue, had occupied the premises at 1189 Albany avenue. One of his children had the small-pox there, and recovered without the fact becoming known to the board of health; then another son was taken ill, and the family removed to 1117 Albany avenue, where the second child died of small-pox. After the undertaker moved out of 1189, John Smethoma moved in, occupying the same flat, which had not been fumigated, and using for a shop a room to which the undertaker's family had free access throughout their illness.

Dr. Brand had notified Smethoma to hold the goods until further notice.

May 15 Inspectors Kelley and Bisno went to 1189 Albany avenue and found the shop empty and locked, and Smethoma sitting in the street in front. He denied that he had had any work within four months, and said that before Christmas he worked for A. L. Singer & Co. At this office his name was found upon the list of Singer's employes. The firm was then notified as follows:

Messrs. A. L. Singer & Co., 168-170 Market Street, Chicago.

GENTLEMEN:—There is small-pox at 1189 Albany avenue, where one Smethoma is working for your house. There has been infection on these premises since April 1, at least; one death and a series of small-pox cases. Day before yesterday, goods in process of manufacture were found in the shop, and the man was ordered not to remove them until they had been disinfected. This morning we find that the goods are gone. They must have been returned to you, or left in some other place—perhaps secreted in another equally infected place.

Kindly let us know by bearer if these goods have been returned to you, and if you have any other goods made up by this man, in your stock. To prevent the spread of infection the goods the man has disposed of must be found and taken care of in the proper manner.
Yours very truly,
FLORENCE KELLEY.

The following reply to this letter was brought back by Inspector Hickey:

A. P. Stevens, Assistant Factory Inspector:

We have not received any work from Smethoma, 1189 Albany street, since April 26. We will find out if expressman delivered any work this week.   Respectfully yours,
A. L. SINGER & CO.

Later the following was received from this firm, on the same date (May 15):

A. P. Stevens, Assistant Factory Inspector:

Since your man called here this afternoon, we have found that the express man delivered to Smethoma, 1189 Albany avenue, twenty-three men's coats and twenty-seven children's coats, on the 11th inst.

Respectfully yours,

A. L. SINGER & CO.

May 16—Mr. A. L. Singer brought Smethoma to this office to state where the Singer goods were secreted. At this time Smethoma's own child lay dead of small-pox at 1189 Albany avenue, the death occurring this morning. Inspector Hickey went with Smethoma to see where the goods were hidden, and reported that they were in barrels, packed in the loft of a barn or shed on premises at 1189 Albany avenue, with empty barrels piled on top of those in which the goods were hidden. Inspector Hickey reported, also, that on the way to locate the goods the man Smethoma entered two drug stores looking for a doctor to make arrangement for the burial of his child, although, as he informed Inspector Hickey, he had not had his clothes off, nor had he washed, for three days, during which he had tended the child now dead.

At 3 o'clock on this day (May 16) the Singer goods in Smethoma's 'possession were burned by an agent of the Board of Health, in Inspector Hickey's presence, and with a mob of Smethoma's neighbors surging about the place. On this day the records of the board of health show that there were three new cases of small-pox at 1189 Albany avenue. To this date there had been at no time any effort to quarantine the place.

May 29.—Smethoma came to this office to get permission to resume work, and produced the following certificate:

May 28, 1894.

To whom it may concern:

This is to certify that the store of 1189 Alabamy avenue has been fumigated on May 17, and no more small-pox exists about the place. He can be allowed to resume business. W. E. MILLER, M. D.,

Med. Inspector of Health Department.

The health department records show three cases of small-pox at this number May 17, and one new case on May 22, again in the family of Smethoma, the tailor. Including the two cases in the undertaker's family, which were not made a part of the health department's records, there were seven cases of small-pox, at least two fatal, on these premises in May, yet this shop certificate was issued by a city district physician that work could be resumed there during that month. It can hardly be needful to state that this permission to resume work was not endorsed by this office.

The history of this shop is the history of the fatal concealments incident to tenement house manufacture. The undertaker concealed from the board of health the fact that small-pox was in his family. The incoming tenant, Smethoma, was therefore not warned that there had been small-pox in the family of the outgoing tenant, the undertaker. Smethoma in turn concealed from A. L. Singer & Co., for whom he worked, the fact that there was small-pox in his family on May 16, and concealed their work on his premises from the State factory inspectors.

When it is considered that there has been, throughout the epidemic in the Bohemian sweat-shop district, concealed cases of small-pox, so many that the district physician in charge once stated to an inspector his belief that there were at that moment not less than 500 cases within a radius of six blocks, the painful conviction forces itself upon us that the Smethoma case is typical of many, which, with all our efforts, we failed to reach.

May 15, 1894—John Vancura, 436 W. 17th street, coat-maker for L. Abt & Co.. 218 Market street. Inspectors Kelley and Bisno.

On this date between 9 and 10 p. m., the inspectors found small-pox in this tenement house, a women to ill to be moved, in the rear basement, and the yellow card on the door. Directly over the patient's room is Vancura's shop, where the full number of employés had worked throughout the day. Three of these employés live on the premises, as do Vancura and his family. There are three families in the house, one living adjacent to the infected family on the ground floor, and Vancura occupying the entire upper floor for his home and shop, which are not separated. The inspectors found two of Vancura's children sleeping in a room next to the shop, with the door open between the rooms. The arms of the sleeping children were not examined by the inspectors but Vancura had no vaccination certificates for them. There were thirty-four overcoats in process of manufacture in his shop.

May 16—an order was served on Commitsioner Reynolds to condemn and destroy the goods in Vancura's shop in accordance with § 2 of the work-shop law. Inspector Bisno accompanied Dr. Henry Reynolds to the shop. Vancura complained to Dr. Harry Reynolds of the failure to quarantine the family where the small-pox was, that the members of the family were in and out, doors and windows were open, and consequently his own family was exposed to the infection. Dr. Henry Reynolds did not, however, remove or destroy the goods in Vancura's shop, but went away saying that he would return with a police force and take the goods the next day.

May 17—Inspectors Kelley and Stevens visited Vancura's shop and found the goods gone and the shop empty. They were informed that "a man with a buggy" had taken the goods away. The small-pox patient was still on the premises. At no time on the 15th, 16th or 17th of May was any quarantine maintained here.

L. Abt & Sons reported that Dr. Henry Reynolds had taken these goods which had been ordered destroyed to be sterilized, a distinct violation of § 2 of the Workshop law.

May 16, 1894—Joseph Triska, 691 Alport street, contractor for Cahn, Wampold & Co.. 209-210 Monroe street. Inspectors Kelley and Stevens.

This shop is in the rear basement of a tenement house, Triska living on the premises. The inspectors found the shop locked and looking through the widow, ascertained that it was empty. There were two cases of small-pox in Triska's family. One daughter, Mary, then lay dead in the house, and another child had just been taken to the pest-house. The yellow card was on the door and a policeman was on guard. From a woman in the house the inspectors learned that goods had been removed from the shop that day. Neither the officer nor any one else present knew who removed the goods, nor by what authority it was done, nor where they had been taken. Inspector Kelley telephoned Cahn, Wampold & Co., and was informed by them that the goods from Triska's shop had been taken to the sterilizers by agents of the city health department.

The cases of small-pox in Triska's family were not diagnosed as such until the night preceding this inspection, but the condition of the victims made it manifest that the disease had been present for some days before. How much clothing was manufactured in and removed from this shop during this period, the inspectors had no means of ascertaining.

May 19, 1894—Mary Griffen, 686 S. Paulina street, shirts and boys' waists for Hyman, 237 Monroe street. Inspectors Kelley and Bisno.

The inspectors found Mrs. Griffin in a ground floor front room of a tenement house. Mother, daughter and granddaughter live, cook, sleep and work in this one room. The mother had twenty-eight boys' waists in the room, in process of manufacture for Hyman. The inspectors made a careful search of the premises and found the yellow card posted on the second floor rear door. They learned that a child had been taken sick several days before, but that the diagnosis of the case as small-pox was not made until Friday afternoon, May 18, when the district physician promised that the patient should be removed to the pest-house within twenty-four hours. At the time of this inspection the twenty-four hours had elapsed, but there were no preparations for the removal of the child. Mrs. Griffin was notified not to remove the waists until further notice.

May 20—Sunday—Inspectors Kelley and Bisno again visited this house, at noon. The child had been removed about one hour before, and a promise had been given that the place should be fumigated on Monday morning.

May 21—Premises at 686 S. Paulina street were fumigated late in the afternoon, including Mrs. Griffin's room with boys' waists.

May 23—Permission was given to remove the boys' waists from Mrs. Griffin's room, but not to take more work to the same place until it was seen whether there was a recurrence of the disease there, as seemed more than probable from the delay in dealing with the case.

May 22, 1894—Anton Randa, 1636 W. 22nd street, custom tailor for Kelley Bros., merchant tailors, 268 S. State street. Inspector Bisno.

The inspector found Randa's shop in his living rooms in a cottage basement. There were nine people in the family, five of whom, Randa's wife and four of his children, were sick with small-pox. The four small rooms are used for eating, sleeping, living and manufacturing, and in the room used for a shop are two machines, three chairs, two tables and one bed. No goods were found in the shop, nor was Randa there, but, as the inspector was informed by Randa's child, he had gone after more work. The five small-pox patients were at this time in the house.

At 8 p. m. the inspector returned to Randa's house, found him, and learned that the patients had been removed to the pest-house. Randa at first insisted that he had not had any work for six months, but finally admitted that he worked for Kelley Bros., 268 S. State street, that he had delivered to them a coat very recently, and that he had also taken from them one coat to make on this day, May 22nd. Where this coat was he absolutely refused to tell, nor could Inspector Bisno find it on the premises.

May 23—Inspector Stevens went to the store of Kelley Bros. Neither of the partners was there. This case was reported, as above, to their cutter, and an order on Randa for the coat in his possession was obtained. This cutter also told Inspector Stevens that the other coat had been returned by Randa on Thursday, May 17th, and had been ,delivered to a customer. The inspector asked for the name and address of this customer, which the cutter claimed not to know.

An order was issued for Commissioner Reynolds to destroy, in accordance with § 2 of the workshop law, any goods in process of manufacture found in Anton Randa's possession. Inspector Bisno, accompanied by two agents of the board of health. returned to 1636 W. 22d street, and gave Randa the order from Kelley Bros. for the coat. Randa then took them to 1616 W. 22d street, on which premises he had concealed the work, and produced it. They found a boy in the family where this coat was concealed who appeared to have small-pox, and the inspector remained there until a district physician was obtained, who diagnosed the case as small-pox.

The infected coat was then taken to an adjacent vacant lot, and burned by the agents of the board of health in the presence of Inspector Bisno.

—3 S.

The district physician having given his opinion that the coat
returned by Randa to Kelley Bros. on Thursday, May 17, was
undoubtedly in an infectious condition, Inspectors Stevens and
Bisno went to the store of Kelley Bros. to make another attempt to trace the coat. This time one of the partners was in
the store. He was told of the destruction of the coat found
hidden at 1616 W. 22d street, and of the circumstances under
which the coat returned to him on May 17 was made. Inspector Stevens then told Mr. Kelley that the district physician
had decided that this coat also was infected, and again asked
for the name and address of the customer who had received it.
Mr. Kelley replied that the coat was still in the store, and that
he was willing that it should be destroyed. When told that
his cutter had that morning reported the coat as delivered to
a customer, Mr. Kelley replied that this was not so, that the
coat was still in the store.

May 24—An order was issued for Commissioner Reynolds to
destroy this coat, in accordance with § 2 of the Workshop law.
Inspector Bisno went with the two agents of the board of
health to Kelley Bros.' store, where they were given a coat,
which the city agents burned in the presence of Inspector Bisno.

Can the dangers of tenement house manufacture be more
drastically manifested? Randa concealed from the merchant
tailors who gave him the coats, the fact that small-pox was in
his family, although even while he returned work to them and
received more from them, five victims of the disease lay in the
tenement rooms where the work was done. Again, he concealed
the work from the State inspectors, and in so doing exposed it
still further by hiding it in another house where also there was
small-pox.

**May 24, 1894.—Mrs. Case, 172 Coulter street, waist maker for
Strouss, Eisendrath & Drom, 171 S. Canal street. Inspectors
Kelley and Stevens.**

This inspection was made upon a small-pox "suspect" notice.
Nos. 172 and 174 Coulter street form a double, two-story, ram-
shackle tenement house, crowded with tenants and used also as
a boarding house for employes of the 18th street railway
company, the barns of the company being next door. A call
for diagnosis at both these numbers had been made on May
23, but when the inspectors were there, at noon on May 24,
the district physician had not arrived.

The inspectors made a room to room search of these tenements, and found what appeared to be small-pox in an advanced
stage in three instances, one child living at 174 in the Oakland
family, and two children at 172 in the Kellihar family.

In the rooms above the Kellihar family lives Mrs. Case, who
had, on this morning, returned to Strouss, Eisendrath & Drom
a bundle of cotton waists which she made up for them. The
firm was notified of the probable presence of small-pox at 172

Coulter street, and the consequent danger of infection in these waists, and advised that the same be thoroughly boiled.

May 25—The three cases at 172-174 Coulter street were diagnosed by a district physician as small-pox and the patients were removed to the pest house.

This is one of many cases in which the work of the inspectors has been hampered by the absence of a physician. In some cases much precious time has been lost in waiting for a diagnosis of the district physician of the city board of health, where immediate effective action was impossible without it; and in other cases which might have been recognized at once as non-infectious had we had a physician at command. The wording of § 2 of the law implies the need of a physician, for who else can determine in each case whether there is evidence of infectious or contagious disease present in a shop, with authority sufficient to justify the issuing of an order upon the local board of health to condemn and destroy hundreds of dollars worth of goods in the shop?

May 24, 1894.—Bartholomy Bosek, 696 S. May street, coat maker for The American Tailors, Clark and Monroe streets. Inspectors Kelley and Stevens.

This is a home shop, in the tailor's kitchen, second floor of a rear house. There was no work on the premises and Bosek's wife said that he had gone to his employers to return home completed work and get more. There was small-pox in the front house on this lot, the yellow card on the door but there was no quarantine, and children were all over the premises.

May 26—Inspector Bisno visited Bosek's shop and found him at work on a coat for the American Tailors. The firm was notified not to receive the coat until it was sterilized, and to give Bosek no more work until danger of contagion was over. An order was issued for the sterilization of the coat.

Bosek's shop was watched, and he was found without work when there was a recurrence of small-pox at 696 S. May street, on June 11.

May 24, 1894.—Mrs. Kosh, 1007 Hinman street, work for Max Glaser & Co., 157-159 Market street, and for Ederheimer, Stein & Co., Market and Jackson streets. Inspectors Kelley and Stevens.

The inspectors found this a home shop, in Mrs. Kosh's living rooms, the second floor rear of a large tenement house. Mrs. Kosh had no work. A call for diagnosis had been made for a child at 1005 Hinman street on May 23, but twenty-four hours later, at the time of this inspection, the district physician had not reached the case. After the inspection another twenty-four hours elapsed before, on May 25, the official records at the city hall showed two cases of small-pox at 1005 Hinman street.

May 28, 1894.—Charles Pechek, 1118 Van Horn street, coat maker for Ederheimer, Stein & Co., Market and Jackson streets. Inspector Bisno.

This shop is on the first floor of a rear two-story and basement tenement house. There are eleven persons employed, and eighty coats in process of manufacture were found. Pechek was ordered not to remove them, there being two cases of small-pox in the basement of the front house.

May 29—Ederheimer, Stein & Co. were notified of the danger of contagion in these goods, and warned not to receive them until they had been sterilized. An order for their sterilization was issued.

May 29, 1894.—Anton Rehor, 572 Center avenue, coat maker for Hart, Schaffner & Marx, Jackson and Market streets. Inspectors Bisno and Jones.

There is a crowded, double, four-story tenement house on the front of the lot, Nos. 570, 572, and a small-pox patient in one of the families at No. 570. Rehor's shop is in a rear building, second story. The inspectors found the shop closed, and Rehor told them that he had had no work for a year.

Hart, Schaffner & Marx were notified of the danger of infection in this shop, and warned not to give Rehor work until the danger was passed. The records of the firm show that Rehor returned work to them a week before this date.

May 30, 1894.—John Straka, 833 Alport street, contractor for Kohn Brothers, Monroe and Market streets. Inspectors Stevens and Bisno.

This shop is in a rear building, second floor, and there was no work found in it. In the front house, a deep three-story and basement tenement, there was a case of small-pox, no quarantine, and no yellow card. The only sign to be seen on the house was a sign of "Rooms for Rent," which hung in the window of a room on the first floor front.

Kohn Brothers were notified that there was small-pox on these premises, and warned not to give work to Straka.

May 31, 1894.—Mary Vrelna, 757 W. 18th street, home finisher for Wm. Tredor, 914 W. 20th street. Tredor is a contractor for C. P. Kellogg & Co., 167 Franklin street; Kaufman & Bros., 180 Adams street, and the Standard Pants Company, 218, 220 Market street. Inspectors Stevens and Bisno.

Mrs. Vrelna lives and works in rooms in the rear ground floor of a front frame house. On the floor above a woman, with a new-born babe, lay sick with small-pox, too ill to be moved to the pest house. The yellow card was on the door, and a policeman was on guard.

The inspectors found no work for Tredor, and Mrs. Vrelna said that she had had none for three weeks. In her rooms the inspectors found a young girl whose face showed that she had recently recovered from small-pox. She lives in the ground floor front rooms of this house, adjacent to those of Mrs. Vrelna. She told the inspectors that she was sick with small-pox eight weeks before, and had been well enough to be out for four weeks; that no doctor was called for her, and no one but her family and a few neighbors knew of her sickness. She also said that while she was sick Mrs. Vrelna was sewing for Tredor, and Mrs. Vrelna said that this was so.

This successfully concealed case of small-pox with garments making going on in the adjoining rooms throughout the entire seige, will illustrate the futility of attempted "regulation" of tenement house manufacture. Goods made up eight weeks before danger of contagion in them was known to any person authorized to inspect their sanitary condition, had long before the eight weeks elapsed passed through the hands of the contractor and the manufacturer and may have carried contagion to unsuspecting purchasers.

June 4, 1894—Peter Otto, 1011 Van Horn street, pants maker for Cahn, Wampold & Co., 204-210 Monroe street. Inspectors Stevens and Bisno.

This shop is on the first floor rear of a two-story tenement house, and is not properly separated from Otto's living rooms. The inspectors found eight persons working, with small-pox next door, at 1007 Van Horn street (there is no 1009). The addresses of these eight employés, and of Otto's five home finishers, were taken by the inspectors, and all were found to be living on streets where small-pox is now epidemic.

Cahn, Wampold & Co. were acquainted with these facts by Inspector Kelley, and assured her that their work on these premises was not being closed out, and that no more would be given Otto until the danger from small-pox was over.

June 22—Inspector Bisno visited Otto's shop and found five persons still at work there. There had been recurrence of small-pox at 1007 Van Horn street, two patients having been removed to the hospital on June 16. On the 21st of June, the day previous to this inspection, a child of one of Otto's home finishers living at 1040 Van Horn street, had been taken to the pest-house.

The conditions surrounding the work done in this shop during these June weeks were certainly such that no assurance can be given that the clothing there made up has gone to its purchasers free from infection. Yet the inspectors, their appeal to the manufacturers employing Otto having failed of effect, were powerless to stop work in his shop as there was no technical evidence of actual contagion on the premises.

38

June 6, 1894—Joseph Mathous. 469 W. 19th street, coat maker for Nicoll the Tailor, Adams and Clark streets. Inspectors Kelley and Merz.

This shop is in the first floor rear of a three story tenement house, Mathous living on the premises, shop not properly separated from his living rooms. The inspectors found thirteen persons at work, and six coats completed, or in process of manufacture, or in bundles not yet opened. The addresses of the thirteen employés were taken, and it was found that all were living on streets where small-pox was epidemic.

During this inspection a child was removed from 463 W. 19th street to the pest-house, the fifth case taken from that house. The ambulance and the Health Department carriage stood at the door forty minutes, while a crowd gathered, made up of school children, work people from the neighboring shops, and friends of the patient's family. The little patient was finally carried to the ambulance through a surging crowd of primary school children who pressed about the physicians and drivers, eagerly curious to see how the sick child looked. There were no police in sight, and when the patient had been carried away groups of neighbors stood talking of the large number of cases that had occurred in the block, and of the uselesness of precautionary measures, since "small-pox comes from Heaven, and has nothing to do with making scratches on children's arms."

The record of small-pox by streets shows that there have been cases at 463 and 471 W. 19th street; one case at 714 Loomis street; two cases, one resulting fatally, at 715 Loomis; while one man died of the disease on the day of this inspection at 719 Loomis, corner of W. 19th street, opposite Mathous' shop —a total of ten cases, two of them fatal, on three sides of the shop. The bedding used throughout the illness of the patients at 715 Loomis street had been thrown from the rear windows of the house, and was lying rotting beside 471 W. 19th street.

Mathous was instructed to hold the six coats in his shop for disinfection, and Nicoll was notified not to receive them until they had been sterilized.

June 7—Inspectors Kelley and Bisno went again to Mathous' shop, and found that three coats had been held, but the other three had been returned to Nicoll. Nicoll was at once notified that the coats returned to him by Mathous must be sent to the sterilizer (which was done), and that no more goods could safely be sent to this neighborhood until sufficient time had elapsed to give assurance that there would be no recurrence of the disease. The coats remaining in Mathous' shop were also sterilized.

June 6, 1894.—Anton Benesek, 570 Laflin street, buttonhole maker for a large number of sweat-shops in the infected district. Inspectors Bisno and Merz.

This shop is in the ground floor front of a tenement house. While the inspection was being made a child was carried away from the house next door, dead of black small-pox. The house beyond that in which the child died also had the yellow card out, and two cases of the disease, the patients still in the house. The inspectors found in Benesek's shop twenty-four coats for Shofel, 930 W. 18th street, belonging to Hart, Schaffner & Marx; thirty coats for Mydlil, 444 W. 19th street, also belonging to Hart, Schaffner & Marx; three coats for Prucha, 558 W. 19th street, belonging to L. Arnheim, 175 S. Clark street, and several coats for Bombas, 862 S. Ashland avenue.

The inspectors telephoned to this office for instructions, and an order was issued that all goods then in the buttonhole shop should be sterilized. Before the wagon of the sterilizer reached 570 Laflin street the goods for Mydlil and Shofel had been returned to their shops, which are both in crowded tenement houses in the infected district. The goods were followed to the shops, and taken thence to the sterilizer, and the garments remaining in the buttonhole shop were also sent to be serilized. (In connection with these goods of Hart, Schaffner and Marx, see record of the same Mydlil, May 9th and 16th.)

June 28, 1894—Frank Pospichal, 644 W. 18th street, coat maker for L. Lowenstein & Co., 122 Franklin street. Inspectors Bisno and Moran.

This shop is on the third floor rear of a tenement house. Pospichal's family living on the floor below. In the third floor front a child in a family named Voshlik died of small-pox on June 26, and was taken away for burial on June 27. The inspectors found no work in Pospichal's shop, and he told them that his last work was taken back to Loewenstein & Co. on Friday, June 22d. He also told the inspectors that the child who died of small-pox on June 26 was not taken sick until Monday, June 25.

The account of the firm's transactions with outside contractors showed that Pospichal did return work to them, L. Loewenstein & Co., on June 22, and also that he still had work out for the firm. This work having been exposed to infection, and not being in Pospichal's shop, as the inspectors had seen, Inspector Bisno required an order for it from Mr. Loewenstein, which was given. With the agent of the city sterilizer, he then went with the order to Pospichal, who took them next door, to 646 W. 18th street, and there, in a basement occupied by a Mr. Skala, they found Loewenstein's goods in bundles, 19 in all. These bundles, alleged to contain 13 overcoats and 27 sack coats, were taken to the sterilizer. Pospichal told the inspectors that these goods were taken from his shop to this basement on Tuesday, June 26, the day the child died.

June 29—Inspectors Kelley and Bisno called upon the district physician who had attended the child, Dr. Strzyzowsky, who told them that the Voshlik family were regular patients of his, but, suspecting that the child was ill with small-pox, and fearing that he would order it sent to the pest-house, they had concealed the case and refrained during nine days from calling him in until, the child's death being imminent, they sent for him late on the night of Monday, June 25. When he called again, the following morning, the child was dying.

As the child's entire period of illness was spent in the room adjoining Pospichal's workroom, the Voshlik family and the employes of Pospichal using the same stairs, halls and water closets throughout these nine days, the inspectors decided that the goods returned to Loewenstein & Co. during the illness must be regarded as infectious. They were therefore ordered sent to the city sterilizer before noon on June 29. and were taken thither by the city agent in the presence of Inspector Bisno.

This case, like many of the preceding ones, illustrates the hopelessness of the attempt to guarantee freedom from contagion while tenement house manufacture is tolerated. Here, too, the concealment practiced by the family of the sick child and by the sweater involved the sending out of infectious goods in spite of the infection law. So long as garments are made in homes disease in these homes will be concealed.

Concealments in Tenement Houses.

Among the reasons for concealment, the chief are the fear of the pest-house and financial loss. Parents dread to see suffering little children carried away to a pest-house where 70 per cent. of all the patients die. and they resort to extraordinary measures, such as hiding sick children in coffee-sacks, locking them in water-closets, or smuggling them away to remote suburbs wrapped as bundles of coats and transported in street-cars filled with unsuspected fellow-passengers. In some cases an entire flat has been darkened and locked for days together, the parents coming and going in the small hours of the night, while they nursed their children through the plague, and neighboring tenants upon the same floor believed that the whole family had gone away. In other cases. doors and windows were barricaded as well as locked and bolted, and the health officers were obliged to break down the doors. The afflicted families found steadfast allies in their struggle for concealment among the neighbors whose interest in the matter coincided with their own. Landlords dread the yellow card lest it cause their tenants to flee and hinder new ones from coming. Shop-keepers lose their trade where small-pox is known to be overhead, or in the rear of the shop, and fellow-tenants fear for their goods and their chances of employment, if the presence of the disease is made known and fumigation and quarantine follow.

All these things happen in greater measure during an epidemic than at other times, but on the other hand, public attention is then fixed upon the infectious district, and some precautionary measures are taken. At all times we have with us diphtheria, scarlet fever, measles, typhoid, tuberculosis, scabies and other forms of infectious or contagious disease. The same concealment is practiced, but public scrutiny is lacking, and the danger inherent in tenement manufacture is therefore a permanent one.

Concealments by the City Board of Health.

After June 10 the board of health adopted an avowed policy of concealment. From this time the lists of new cases, which had before been imperfect from a lack of system and of responsible book-keeping, were rendered absolutely worthless by order of the commissioner of health. District physicians were notified to give out no more information, and the city hall lists were reduced to two cases per day. One example of suppression of cases may serve to show how far this policy has been carried. Since it was inaugurated three children of the McLaughlin family, living in a tenement house at 82 Brown street, were removed to the pest-house on three different days. None of three cases appears upon any list. One omission may be explained away as accidental, but not three in the same family, the same house and the same month.

Throughout the epidemic there has been no mortality record by days or weeks, from which we might have formed at least an estimate of the varying degree of danger. Admissions and discharges at the pest-house are known only to the Sister in charge of them, and the daily number has at no time been obtainable from the health department.

The yellow card which would be of inestimable use to us if posted and kept in place upon infectious premises, as prescribed by the city ordinance, has been tacked upon rear sheds and in hallways, upon inside doors, up three flights of stairs and in many cases has never been posted at all. Cards have been torn down in scores of cases but not one prosecution has been instituted by the board of health for this serious offense against the public safety. Trade has been carried on in groceries, milk depots, cigar shops and drug stores, while the warning card was either gone altogether or carefully concealed in an upper story or a rear yard, and customers, ignorant of their danger, visited the infected premises as usual. From this connivance of the local officials at the infamy of landlords and shopkeepers, the State inspectors have suffered with the rest of the community, finding cases too late to take any effective measures for the enforcement of the law, and often failing altogether to learn of the presence of small-pox until weeks after the burial of the patient. And this in spite of faithful daily searching in the infectious district.

The guarding against recurrence of the disease on the same premises with garment-making has been further hindered by the removal of the yellow card immediately after fumigation. Where a patient was removed in the morning and the premises were fumigated and the card removed in the afternoon, an inspector calling an hour later would find no hint of danger and a sweater might go on with his work the next day undisturbed.

The Lesson of the Epidemic.

The presence of a shop in a tenement house adds three elements of danger during an epidemic. It gathers together men, woman and children from other tenements where the disease may be, and instead of keeping them by themselves in large, light factory rooms, the tenement house shop throws them into direct contact with tenants living in the most unwholesome conditions, for the shops are in the worst and most unwholesome houses. Thus the presence of a shop in a tenement house increases the probability that the tenants may have the disease brought to them. And the larger the number of employés coming from other tenement houses the greater this probability.

On the other hand, if the shop is itself in an infected house, the employés can not know the fact in time to save themselves from exposure, for, as has been repeatedly pointed out, many cases have been recognized as small-pox only after the death of the patient.

The third element of danger is the sending out of infectious garments among the unsuspecting purchasing public, which needs no further comment in this report.

The sanitary value of the concentration of the garment-workers in factories which could be permanently located, and successfully inspected, is wholly beyond computation even in ordinary times when there is no epidemic. This consideration alone, would, in the opinion of the inspectors, justify the prohibition of tenement manufacture, as a strictly sanitary measure.

The preceding record of cases illustrates both the protection afforded the public by the law as it stands, and also the weak points of the law, which would have to be amended if the attempt to regulate tenement manufacture by restrictive provisions were to be carried farther. In the opinion of the inspectors, however, this record shows the hopelessness of the attempt to protect the public health from dangers which are inherent in tenement manufacture, and can not be successfully minimized or eradicated while that is tolerated, but can be removed only by its prohibition.

To continue the toleration of manufacture in tenement houses in the face of this year's epidemic would argue the people of Illinois incapable of learning from experience.

RECORD BY STREETS.

The following record of small-pox by streets is compiled from the records of the city board of health, with the addition of cases found by the inspectors through the district physicians' lists of diagnoses, and, finally, by their own search for infection in connection with clothing.

The record is not to be regarded as showing the actual amount of small-pox in juxtaposition to garment-workers, but merely as showing what was ascertained under many and varying difficulties, in a few of the streets in which garment-makers live and work.

The streets selected lie between Sixteenth on the north, and the Chicago River on the south; Fisk street on the east, and the city limits on the west. Those streets within this district have been omitted from the list which exhibited few garments or few cases of small-pox, unless the two were suggestively near together.

Cigar makers, shirt makers, home-finishers, custom tailors, etc., have been indicated as such. All names not otherwise specified indicate sweat-shops, the employés varying in number from one to fifty. In considering the juxtaposition of the cases and the shops, it should be borne in mind that the employés ordinarily live on the same premises, or next door, or in the same block, and always within walking distance; that the shops are in the most crowded houses, and that quarantine and isolation are unknown.

Albany Avenue.

Small-Pox.	Tenement House Shop.
999...............................June 4	
	1046, Mrs. Rothkovska, home-finisher.
1083, Wilfzorck..............April 28	
1095, Rinnac................April 28	
1095, Rinnac, 5 cases..........May 11	
1117, Dizek...................June 1	
1126, Marvin.................June 4	
1133.......................April 16	1133, M. Kubal, custom tailor.
	1147, Rosa Trouble, shirt maker.
	1147, Mrs. Jendel, shirt maker.
1159.......................June 8	
	1166, J. Hestha.
1169.......................May 23	

Albany Avenue—Concluded.

Small-Pox.	*Tenement House Shop.*
1189, Smethoma.............May 16	1189, John Smethoma,coat maker for A. L. Singer & Co., 168 Market st.
1189, Sropahg.................May 17	
1189, Vanacek,2 cases........May 17	
11x9, Smethoma..............May 22	
1193.........................June 5	
1201, Johanek................May 3	
1206.........................June 8	
	1210, M.Williams, contractor for Cahn, Wampold & Co., 204-210 Monroe st., and M. J. Berkson, 234-236 Fifth av.
1213.........................May 20	
1214, Berner................June 4	

Alport Street.

662, Kossel ....May 31	
	663, A. Vaneschek, coat maker for Hirsch, Elson & Co., 160,162 Market st.
	663, J. Dvorak.
665, Olisar ....April 18	665, A. Horky, contractor for M. Born & Co., 250 Market st.
665, Olisar ....April 22	
665, Varbeck ....May 12	
	666, C. Pehore, custom tailor.
	666, A. Thuma, contractor for Cahn, Wampold & Co.
667, Roth, 2 cases ....April 26	
	668, J. Zuich.
	670, J. Suchan.
	677, J. Bauer.
	679, J. Slap-h.
	685, Frank Prybll.
	689, J. Marsalek.
691, Triska, 2 cases........May 15	691, Jos. Triska, contractor for Cahn, Wampold & Co., 204-210 Monroe st.
699, Voncura, 2 cases........May 1	699, Peter Zituek, coat maker for E. Rothschild & Bro., 203,205 Monroe st.
699, Henic..................May 3	
699, Hossm-nn...............May 11	
711, Linehart...............May 3	
711, Jaker..................May 3	
729, Varos..................May 12	
736, Darradl................April 26	
739, Uobelafsky,2 cases.....May 17	
741,........................April 22	
	744, Mrs. Vanicek, shirt maker.
	745, Mrs. Yndacek, shirt maker.
749, Kominlk................May 17	
756, 2 cases................April 20	756, Simon Marsalek, coat maker for Kuh Nathan & Fischer, Franklin and VanBuren sts.
756, Priff, 2 cases..........May 18	
757, Resata.................May 28	757, V. Meazek, contractor for Ederhelmer, Stein & Co., cor. Market and Jackson sts.
	763, L. Hasek, custom tailor.
764, Hart...................May 28	
766, Zarek,2 cases...........May 12	766, N. Kubergnight,* finisher for Benedict, Goldman & Co., 237,239 Market st.
	770, J. Libera.
774, Moravlgz, 2 cases.......May 17	
776, Sechranska.............April 26	
	777, W. Kubin.
778, Seclzy.................April 30	
	779, J. Dvorak.
783, Koracek................June 21	783, Doubovsky, overall maker for Louis Goodman, 156, 158 Market st.
	785, A. Skudliske, custom tailor.
787, Jllma..................April 26	
788, Seclzy.................April 30	
	792, Miss Kohut, home-finisher.
	793, T. Zlk, coat maker.
800, Topka..................April 24	
803, Peha...................May 17	
804, Kucera.................May 1	804, M. Kuech, cigarmaker.
	807, Mrs. Younger, home-finisher.
	816, L. Noseck.
	810, J. Krisl.
	823, Mrs. Kozleh, finisher.
	824, Svoboda.
823, Slava..................May 1	
823, Tafvanek...............May 1	
	830, A. Adler, custom tailor.

* A person who works in the factory by day and carries home goods to finish at night.

Alport Street—Concluded.

Small-Pox.	Tenement House Shop.
833, ...May 30	833, John Straka, contractor for Kohn Bros., Monroe and Market sts.
	840, J. Peseck, custom tailor.

Ambrose Street.

56, ...June 11	
	175, J. Kuhns.
	183, John Metzger.
528, ...April 24	
542, Kich, 2 cases......May 7	
	547, V. Rezab.
582, Englehardt, 2 cases ...April 27	
591, Engel......April 27	
591, Engel, 4 cases......May 7	
591, ...May 19	

South Center Avenue.

	538, John Krecl.
	538, John Nicelik.
	546, Mrs. Vanecek, home finisher.
	556, J. Newman.
	556, F. Matousek.
	565, J. Nieman.
	565, C. Drache, custom tailor.
	567, Mrs. Meushal, shirt maker.
569......April 22	
570......May 29	
	572, A. Rehor, coat maker for Hart, Schaffner & Marx, Jackson and Market sts.
	583, Chas. Smola, cigar maker.
589, Hubka......May 3	
	595, John Bowzek.
	601, Mrs. Spatz, home finisher.
611, Smith......May 11	
	615, Mary Mytler, shirt maker.
	638, J. Schmidt, custom tailor.
	643, J. Denemark.
644......May 18	
674, Weisman......May 11	
	683, Mrs. Kryasovska, shirt maker.
	700, Mrs. Burton, shirt maker.

West Eighteenth Street.

	380, Jacob Herda.
381, Wiltshire......April 22	
381......May 17	
	385, L. Rychavy.
390......June 11	
	417, K. Sickra, cigar maker.
	419, John Kolar, cigar maker.
424, Konwoberika......May 11	
	433, Mary Novobna, shirt maker.
	434, Mrs. Wesser, home finisher.
	435, Mrs. Hossmann, home finisher.
	435, Mrs. Pollnshek, home finisher.
	435, Mrs. Weierick, home finisher.
	436, K. Nebzensky.
	437, Mrs. Novakovska, pants maker.
	461, J. Eppstein, cigar maker.
467, Vaclav Kosatka......May 13	
	471, Vaclav Polka, cigar maker.
	485, Mariska.
	485, A. Jerman, home finisher.
	512, Jos. Hacha, cigar maker.
	514, Soupel Bros.
515, Westerlik......May 11	
	521, Jos. Felipe.
	531, F. Hoby, cigar maker.
	537, Mrs. Miduna, home finisher.
	567, J. Heonlschek.
	569, J. Bauer.
	572, S. Lacina.

West Eighteenth Street—Continued.

Small-Pox-	Tenement House Shop.
575, Westerlik.................May 11	
	580, F. Coaz.
	588, J. Vavricek, cigars.
	589, S. Skokal.
599, Wistein ....May 16	
	601, Wm. Feruka, cigarmaker.
	604, Joe Hondek.
	608, A. Fiala.
	626, J. Novak.
	627, J. Dvorak, custom tailor.
644, Voshlik....................June 26	644, Frank Pospichal, contractor for L. Loewenstein & Co., 122 Franklin st.
	648, J. Tuma.
	650, Mrs. Rawhicb, home finisher.
651, Bandor ....June 22	
	653, Jos. Blaha.
	680, Jos. Kalina, cigar maker.
682, Helm ....March 13	
683, Hovish...................May 12	
690, Stochouska.............May 28	
	691, F. Rehon, shirt maker.
692, Perozinska, 2 cases.....May 15	
692, Perozinska ....May 28	
694 ....May 25	
694, Prezek ....June 2	
697.........................June 11	697, F. Partie, custom tailor.
702.........................June 11	
704, Wisniewski.............May 11	704, David Schwartz, cloak maker for F. Siegel & Bros., 222-228 Market st., also for Mannheimer, Lepman & Co., 221 Market st.
704, Szumski, 2 cases ....May 15	
704, Machezewski...........May 15	
704, Guinot, 3 cases ....May 15	
704, Keri, 4 cases ....May 15	
707, Lesceyk...............April 22	
707, Lesceyk...............April 30	
707, Lesceyk.................May 2	
714.........................May 15	
	715, Worda.
	717, J. H. Daniel, cigar maker.
718, Severson................June 20	
719.........................April 22	
720.........................April 21	723, M. Belinsky, contractor for Joseph Belfeld & Co., 253 Jackson st.
721, Zamadski ....April 30	
723 ....May 2	723, J. Daketin, home finisher for W. Franz, 927 W. 17th contractor for Kuh, Nathan & Fischer, cor. Franklin and VanBuren sts.
724, Miniewskorsky, 2 cases.May 16	
726.........................May 14	
728 ....May 17	
	731, Trumak, custom tailor.
	734, Joseph Hantak, cigar maker.
	737, Anton Stengl, cigar maker.
741, Bolardofsky ....May 15	
745, Chria ....April 30	745, J. Dvorak, contractor for Strauss, Yondorf & Rose, cor. Market and Quincy sts.
757, Ceskl ....May 28	757, Mary Vrina, home finisher for Wm. Tredor, 914 W. 20th st., a contractor for C. P. Kellogg & Co., 167 Franklin st.; Kauffmann Bros., 180 Adams st., and The Standard Pants Co., 218-220 Market st.
772, Schole..............April 16	
773, Naymann ....May 3	
774.........................April 23	774, Mrs. Showers, home finisher for Carl Heider, 937 W. 18th st., a contractor for E. Rothschild & Bro., 203-205 Monroe st.
775, 2 cases ....April 22	
775, Rutkowski............April 27	
775, Kulder.................May 15	
	780, J. Serpan.
781, Koveris................April 28	
786, Mravek.................May 11	
	800, F. Novak, home finisher.
	800, A. Straud, home finisher.
	816, M. Vancura, home finisher.
	822, J. Skansky, home finisher.
	830, F. Martinek.
	832, A. Jarganska.
834.........................June 7	834, J. Bosinsky, contractor for Becker, Meyer & Co., 218-220 Market st.
	862, J. Korar.
	866, Mrs. Swonda, home finisher.
	866, J. Haydonek.

West Eighteenth Street—Concluded.

Small-Pox.

902, Knaack.................April 18
902, Knaack.................April 22
905, Knaack.................May 10
905, Keffner...............May 16
905, Kerriher, 2 cases ....May 16
911, Podonak...............May 16
916, Lubvo.................May 12

932, Benke.................May 5

Cor. 18th st. and Hoyne av..
Benef ....May 9

979, Beleck................April 28
979, Beleck, 2 cases..........May 15
983, Pokorney ....April 22
987.........................May 28
997.........................May 16
1006.......................April 26

Tenement House Shop.

906, Parath, home finisher.
913, Mrs. Strinkowska, home finisher.
917, Mrs. Pokersky, home finisher.
920, Vrosha.
920, G. Polega.
926, Jangelska, home finisher.
927, A. Bogda.
930, J. Soufel.
930, L. Skivhardt.
931, Mrs. Dahlms, home finisher.
937, Chas. Heider.
939, Richard Willer.
941, Miss Dahms, home finisher.
957, John Geceuartz.
975, Mrs. Shelta, home finisher.
1006, Johanna Asetta, home finisher.
1006, B. Beyer, home finisher.

Eighteenth Place.

115, Sriener................April 30
148, Haines ....April 30
148, Karmaleck.............May 8

113, Harda, custom tailor.
147, Willer, home finisher.
148, Kubesh, home finisher.

Fisk Street.

71, Jrenek ....May 18
71, Jormalek...............May 18

110, Berlik................May 4
110, Berlik................May 8

23, Mrs. Koshner, home finisher.
39, E. Korn.
59, J. Hrabak.
60, M. Ciesal.
60, C. Dome!. ·
80, Mrs. Maschkora, home finisher.
88, Barbara Schala, home finisher.
96, J. Budilorsky.
96, J. Honda.
97, J. Lacina.
97, J. Voetrocky.
115, M. Kolar, cigars.
119, J. Fikesch, custom tailor.

Hinman Street.

895, Stuler................June 19
929, Wallin...............May 10

1005, Saltaor, 2 cases ....May 25

864, Miss Ford, shirt maker.
908, Mary Solinkmann, finisher.
929, J. Frick, contractor for L. Loewenstein & Co., 122 Franklin st.
943, Sophie Schueler, finisher.
943, F. Schultz, finisher.
955, Annie Kroning, finisher.
957, Annie Michaels, finisher.
1007, Mrs. Kosh.

Hinman Street—Concluded.

Small-Pox.	Tenement House Shop.
1028 ....Aɲril 22	
	1039, H. Edelman, finisher.
	1094, *Chas. Grube*, cigars.
	1125, Minnie Otto, finisher.
1132, Kohung ....May 1ᵒ	
1138, Gai te.................May 10	
	1221, L. Srighardt.
1232, Dolezal.................May 30	
	1257, E. Figalis.
1264..........................June 11	
	1295, J. Kondellea.
	1315, K. Killian.
1331, Melka, 2 cases...........May 1	

Laflin Street.

	53ᵒ, J. Kabacek, custom tailor.
	568, J. Raska.
	570, A. Beheschek, buttonholer.
	571, Thomas Sasek.
	573, Mrs. Lawrence, shirt maker.
574, Slepizka...............June 6	574, Mrs. Salwich, shirt maker far A. Lewin & Sons, 187
574...........................June 11	Market st.
576, Vavnum, 2 cases.........May 2ᵒ	576, Mrs. Broknap, finisher.
	576, Mrs. Smallinsky, home finisher for A. Lewin & Son, 187 Market st.
	578, Mrs. Becha, shirt maker.
582............................June 1	582, Mary Pecha, overall maker for A. Lewin & Sons,187 Market st.
689, Ondrak ....Feb. 7	

South Leavitt Street.

	834, Broysha, home finisher.
	925, Edward Kamies.
	933, M. Zellner.
961.......................Feb. 24	
1037, Stens................June 25	
	1039, *Jos. Weiler*, cigars.
1083.......................June 11	
	1133, Mrs. Douhbke, shirts.
	1200, F. Carson.

Loomis Street.

	616, Mrs. Wahlteick, shirt maker.
	636, Joe Brousek.
	636, *Chas. Skoupy*, cigar maker.
	640, Mrs. Hobka, home finisher.
	646, James Shofel.
	670, Mrs. Sweska, home finisher.
	675, Jos. Sanger, custom tailor.
	675, Chas. Laska.
677..........................June 8	677, Annie Hendina, home stitcher for Louis Goodman & Son, 156-158 Market st.
	695, John Chleboun.
700, Harmach................May 3	
	703, Frank Motls.
714, Smith..................June 7	
715, Perlinsky..............April 30	
715..........................May 14	
	718, *J. Wellfish*, cigars.
719, Galler.................June 6	
719, Galler.................June 25	
	722, Frank Prepeschal.
	722, J. Jilk.
	722, Matousek.
	723, *G. Rokus*, cigar maker.
727..........................June 6	727, John Cuchne, contractor for E. Rothschild & Co., 203-205 Monroe st.
727, Cregis ....Juhe 27	731, Mrs. Coysoyed, shirts.
	740, M. Dvorak, cigars.
742 ....April 16	
742, Duc....................May 3	743, Mrs. Fidehlp, shirts.
	756, Mrs. Siek, shirts.

Marvin Street.

Small-Pox.

33, Kravetzky..............April 28
:═ ●—
234, Dolezal, 2 cases..........May 3
240, Kezel ....June 4

Tenement House Shop.

42, C. Erickson, custom tailor.
232, J. Beranek, custom tailor.

245, Albert Mayer, custom tailor.
247, Jos. Cerny, custom tailor.
248, John Kocka, custom tailor.

South May Street.

652, Martinek, 2 cases.......May 13
●
672, Kazin ....May 15
.0311

696, Ecek ....May 18
696, ...May 24
696, ...June 11
699, Staw ....May 11
1103, Saukub...............June 6

646, Frank Neosinal, custon tailor.
662, Frank Smith, home finisher.
678, Mrs. Wagausch, finisher.
680, Frank Schuk, coat maker.
680, Mrs. Peters, home finisher.
682, Mrs. Popatka, finisher.
693, A. Sticka, custom tailor.
696, B. Bosek, custom tailor for The American Tailors, Clark and Monroe sts.

West Nineteenth Street.

206, Keating...............April 22
443, Dudas..................May 21

436, Shulda, 2 cases..........May 8

463, Ofchada, 4 cases ....May 16
464, ...June 6

471, ...May 4

562, Krossman ....May 5

628, Harrington ....March 13

646, ...April 22

674, ...June 11

202, A. Havlin.
442, Frank K'ava.
444, Frank Jisa, coat maker for Simon, Leopold & Solomon, 165, 167 Market st.
444, J. Mydlil, coat maker for Hart, Schaffner & Marx, Jackson and Market sts.
450, M. Baumrucker.
450, J. Risnicek.
450, F. Coas.
453, V. Tyler, custom tailor.
458, J Kucera.
460, A. Chmelik.
469, Jos. Matthous, custom tailor for Nicoll the Tailor, Adams and Clark sts.
495, Mrs. Fister, shirts.
501, F. Prucha, custom tailor.
510, Wm. Gavis, custom tailor.
510, B. Kunik.
548, James Kalat.
549, Peter Daruret.
550, Jos. Tourek.
552, Mrs. Jeka, shirts.
557, Mrs. Burman, shirts.
558, F. Prucha.
565, Jos. Hronek.
567, M. Williams.
567, Frank Hrawicka.
567, Bohonek.
568, A. Gepschek.
568, Thos. Kaiser.
587, Mrs. Hengurisch, finisher.
616, Aug. Teski.
639, Mrs. Fremach, shirts.
640, H. Zitnek.
644, Ber. ha Pease.
646, Mrs. Mineschek, shirt maker, working for A. Lowin & Sons, 187 Market st.
654, A. Koslovska, custom tailor.
674, J. Winbach, cigars.
678, Minnie Mohr.
679, A. Bennett.
679, J. Zicek.

—4 S.

West Nineteenth Street—Concluded.

Small-Pox.	Tenement House Shop.

690, Mattor .... May 3

696, ... June 11

732, Witt .... May 8

840, ... May 28
874, ... June 6
874, ... June 9

884, ... Feb. 24

892 .... June 25
894, Freda .... May 31
894, Poukopka .... June 13
897 .... May 9

917, Keonkowsky .... June 7

932, Troula .... May 15

947, Fiklik .... May 17

1020, Hoise .... May 23
1020, Hoise .... June 9

1069 .... April 22
1067 .... April 24
1071, Woise, 2 cases .... March 2

694, Home finisher, name unknown.

700, Mrs. Iatga, home finisher.
702, Mrs. Macly, home finisher.
707, Mary Micka.
707, Mrs. Sass.
764, A. Wenzloff.
834, E. Fighas.

874, Mrs. Wollenberg, home finisher for Chas. Marquardt, 955 Hinman st., contractor for John Harper, 186,188 Fifth av., C. P. Kellogg & Co., 167 Franklin st., Kohn Bros., 144 Market st., L. C. Wachsmuth & Co., 122 Market st.
875, Chas. Dvorak.
879, J. Palka, home finisher.
882, Agnes Schultz, home finisher.
884, A. Pavlovska, finisher for Chas. Marquardt, a contractor for C. P. Kellogg & Co., 167 Franklin st., Kohn Bros., 144 Market st., L. C. Wachsmuth & Co., 122 Market st., and John Harper, 186,188 Fifth av.
885, Frank Vick.
887, Mrs. Patoweka.
889, Frank Soucek.

901, James Chizek, custom tailor for M. Born, 256 Market street.
909, Mike Davit.
910, Annie Rieder, home finisher.
918, M. Darott.
918, Home finisher, name unknown.
920, G. Polega.
921, Frank Pavel.
925, Aug. Bogda.
932, M. Kukelski, home finisher.
935, K. Podelska, home finisher.
942, Mary Drucelska, home finisher.
943, Mary Christni.
943, Joseph Jezek, cigar-maker.
944, B. Krasiwski, home finisher.
644, A. Babit, home finisher.
946, Mrs. Nossorinska, home finisher.
947, Mrs. Dewinska, home finisher for R. Molkentine, 899 W. 20th st., a contractor for John Harper, 186 Fifth av.
949, Mrs. Roogela, home finisher.
954, Annie Rogosonski, home finisher.
964, Mrs. Noswinski, home finisher.
964, V. Jerabek.
966, Mrs. Lucas, shirts.
969, Annie Kocka, home finisher.
947, Emily Roe-ka, home finisher.
979, B. Karithera, home finisher.
984, Agnes Younger, home finisher.
1011, Mrs. Bilk, shirts.
1013, A. Foral, home finisher.
1015, Mrs. Schrofscky.

1023, C. Fox, home finisher.
1031, M. Wrbanski.
1033, Emma Projahn, home finisher.
1037, Mrs. Fronck, home finisher.
1038, Wm. Witt.
1044, Mrs. Kolvinska, home finisher.
1066, Young, custom tailor.

1080, Mary Kadlec, home finisher.
1082, Mary Hicman, home finisher.
1092, J. Petka, home finisher.
1092, Mrs. Vosboeska, home finisher.

51

South Oakley Avenue.

Small-Pox. | *Tenement House Shop.*

1032, Mrs. Arnold. knee-pants.
1062, F. Stoerck, coat-maker.
1081, Mrs. Bariger, home finisher.

1115, Anderson .... May 25
1143, Richter, 2 cases .... April 26

1149, Mrs. Stark, shirt-maker.
1154, *John Pelikanagar.*

1157, Miller .... June 14

1172. *John Slapak*, cigars.
1172, Mrs. Manstrom.

West Seventeenth Street.

405, F. Neraz.
407, J. Prochaska.
415, Frank Krira.
415, Jos. Chalk.
419, Pinta.

426 .... May 4 | 426, E. Bubuck, custom tailor.
431, J. S. Spiral.

436, Smola .... May 15 | 436, John Vanchura, coat maker for L. Abt & Son, 218
436 .... May 17 | Market st.
476, Verrick .... May 1

574, J. Jiracek, custom tailor.
585, Maria Hanslora, shirts.
586, Mrs Decker, shirts.
596, John Foyt.
596, J. Polanka.
614, Mrs. Salensky, home finisher.
625, L. Martinek.
643, J. Cihak.
671, Mrs. Younger, home finisher.

683, Kullmuski, 6 cases .. January 6
689, Schultz .... May 8
690, Trusch, 2 cases .... May 17
682 .... June 3
694 .... June 3
697 .... June 8

698, Mary Donaska, finisher.

700, H. Carach, 3 cases ..... May 2
700, Koluka .... May 2

7?2, Mrs. Blouzek, shirts.

704 .... May 17

711, J. Hollechek, custom tailor.

726, Puetski .... May 7
726, Viseckl, 2 cases .... May 17
732, Hanselke .... March 30
734, Kolacek .... May 2
734, Kolacek .... May 7
734, Kolacek, 3 cases ...... May 15
736 .... May 4
737, Bens .... May 25
739, Zezenski .... May 18
741, Galinska .... May 24
744, Sibek .... June 14
744, Sibek .... June 23
755, Volinsky .... June 13
757, Lenzek, 3 cases ...... April 27

770, *A. Poklop*, cigars.
773, Annie Michalske, finisher.
775, Zezenske .... May 17 | 775, Tyly Richter.
775, Jos. Bouchora, home finisher for Wm. Franz, 927 W. 17th st., contractor for Kuh, Nathan & Fischer, Franklin st., cor. VanBuren.

781, Maiseck, 2 cases .... June 2
783, Mrs. Knutt, home finisher.

785 .... June 25
780, Drysch .... June 2

791, Mrs. Schblablescky, finisher.
796, Krez .... May 5 | 796, John Panushka, tailor.
796, Krez .... May 7 | 796, Jos. Daubek, contractor for Chas. P. Kellogg & Co., Franklin, cor. Monroe st., and O. & L. Nye, 231. Blue Island av.

797, Chuolar .... May 15
797 .... June 8

832, P. Andryschak, finisher.
832, Mrs. Knutkonski, finisher.
833, J. Andryschak, finisher.
838, Mary Salonska, finisher.
839, Frank Vondracek, shirts.
845, C. Hitzman.

West Seventeenth Street—Concluded.

Small-Pox.

849..........................June 8
863, Bambrovska ....March 30
864, Hary Zewska...........April 23
903, Klicka, 2 cases...........May 16
903, Klicka....................May 24
907, Kramp...................May 16
909, Dolezal ....May 11

1293........................ April 24

998, Glasner ....May 29
103', 4 cases.................May 20
1037, Terrey ....April 22
1037, Terrey, 2 cases ....May 10
1047.......................June 11

456, Ellinger..............March 2

695, Pitvacek...................May 7

717..........................June 8
719, Brozok...................May 1
719, Kangarski, 3 cases ......May 1
1311, Shea.................June 18

570...........................May 4

590, Simons..................May 12
604, Leitner ....June 23
605, Stefan ....June 13

640, Braaschashar..........April 22
640.........................June 4
645, Meydrick..............May 12

662......................April 22

667, Omdrach.................May 17

Tenement House Shop.

855, J. Jeracek.

870, Mrs. Tuma, finisher.
902, Socup, custom tailor.

909, F. Parlac, pants maker for Cahn, Wampold & Co., 204-210 Monroe st.
919, Taluzcheck, shirts.
923, Elizabeth Wackman, finisher.
927, Wm. Franz.
939, Rose Hoilka, home finisher.
1274, Mrs. Hens, home finisher.
1267, Mrs. Celer.

1297, Aug. Prieske.

Sawyer Avenue.

1136, J. Hondous, coat maker.
1138, Jos. Stvejic, coat maker.
1282, A. Mesek.

West Sixteenth Street.

83, J. Kas.
387, T. Vina.
403, F. Hruda.
509, Wm. Krahulic.
509, Edmund Just.
535, B. Werthelmer.

705, J. Bozorsky, coat maker for Kuppenheimer & Co., Monroe and Franklin sts.
717, J. Konecy, custom tailor.
717, W. Bolnicki, custom tailor.

Throop Street.

566, J. Moravitz.
568, F. Beckwur, custom tailor.
576, M. Honolka.
578, J. Peschek.
583, Stadeck.
593, J. Richter, cigars.
605, J. Benesek, home finisher.
612, F. Polifka, cigars.
616, F. Balik.
633, J. Venopal.
645, J. Cerenek, custom tailor for A. A. Devore & Sons., Michigan av. and Adams st.
650, A. Herda.
662, J. Formanek, cigars.
665, M. Kalina, cigars.
666, Frank Nerna.
668, Wm. Schmidt, custom tailor.
673, H. Stasny.
673, Barbara Nemicek, woolen shirts.

Small-Pox.	Tenement-House Shop.

689, Jansky....................Jan. 30
705.........................June 11
714, Hotek..................June 14

715, Boucharls.
718....................May 20 718, Mrs. Ramm, home finisher.
718, Bubel..................June 13

721, Mrs. Rudish, home finisher.

Troy Street.

1024, T. Harleck.
1042, M. Pouchakas.
1043, A. Hofriter.
1049, John Friedel.

1070 ....May 4
1072 ....May 25
1072 ....May 30
1097, Palon..................June 6
1103.........................June 9
1107, DeLecke...............May 17
1144, Res, 4 cases...........May 10

1156, L. Hallupa.
1167, Schultz, custam tailor.

1168, Vinge ....April 20
1207, Carney ....June 1

West Twentieth Street.

West from Fisk street.

269, 2 cases.................April 26 269, John Tlka, contractor for M. Born & Co., 256 Monroe st.
321, *John Keliekes*, cigars.
323, B. Steyhal, custom tailor.

346, Rudvicky ....May 29
474, Rovoyny................May 1
483, Cerveny ....May 17
484, Vlata...................May 30

487, Mrs. Wurhamoritz, home finisher.
491, Mrs. Carvenske, home finisher.
499, Mrs. Soper, shirt maker.
500, Frank Zacher.
524, V. Krecek.
539, Vaclav Zaloudek.
539, Ole Hebbe.
544, Mrs. Tismor, shirt maker.
546, J. Baumel, custom tailor.
546, Mrs. J. Tiro, shirts.
547, John Besek.
554, Mrs. Bresaus, shirts.
580, Teos. Vosecky, custom tailor.
611, John Komovous.
617, A. Yefschck.
617, J. Zeitheimer.
652, Mrs. Smith.
655, Mrs. Buesch, shirts and waists.
659, Mrs. Strousk, cloaks.

660, Dania ....May 26
669, Zindel.................June 1
669, Zindel.................June 14
669, Zindel.................June 28

684, L. Greene.
693, *J. Meirdirks*, cigars.

699, 2 cases ....May 4
739, Frank Stasney.
741, *Wm. Rheinfels*, cigars.

774 ....May 25
780, Litzky.................May 15
780 ....May 28

787, M. Boechert.
809, G. Koeller

817.........................June 25
831, Agnes Smith.
856, Herman Gaske, finisher.
856, Fred Gabol, home finisher for Charles Marquardt,
855 Hinman st., a contractor for O. P. Kellogg &
Co., 167 Franklin st., and Kohn Bros., 144 Market
st., and L. C. Wachsmuth & Co., 122 Market st.

856, Kirchoff................April 24
856, Kirchoff................April 30

856, Kirchoff................May 1
857.........................June 12

West Twentieth Street.—Concluded.

Small-Pox.	*Tenement House Shop.*
	858, Wm. Farber, coatmaker for L. C. Wachsmuth & Co., 122 Market st.
	877, Oesterreicher.
	899, R. Molken'ine.
	901, Bertha Burke, home finisher.
910, Heinig ....May 9	911, Mrs. Tierman, home finisher.
	913, Mrs. Knorr, home finisher.
	914, Wm. Treder.
	930, Mrs. Neuser, finisher.
931 ....May 10	
952, Krause ....June 11	
955 ....May 24	
959 ....May 24	
971, Bendin ....May 10	
1009 ....May 4	
1011 ....March 19	969, Jos. Kochauska, finisher.
	1043, W. Willer.
	1068, F. Platz.
	1071, F. Platz.
	1078, S. Haller.
1268 ....May 20	

West Twenty-first Street.

	561, A. Bennett.
	622, *G. B. Tietz*, cigars.
	623, L. Saveske.
Twenty-first and Loomis sts.,	
Johnston...............May 13	
625, Kolka...............April 28	625, Joseph Kolka, sweater coat maker for Pfaelzer, Sutton & Co., Franklin and Van Buren sts.
	629, J. Nemecek.
	656, *J. Freland*, cigars.
	694, J. Titek.
	790, Mrs. Kraft, shirts and waists.
	794, Emile Freytag, finisher.
	818, Minnie Freshke, finisher.
	833, M. Spree, finisher.
	872, *H. Stoefhas*, cigars.
991.......................June 9	
	1003, L. Koch, finisher.
	1006, Chas. Bratzhoff, finisher.
1020, Messer ....May 26	
1020.......................June 6	
	1046, John Neuzel, custom tailor.
	1046, H. Mika, shirt maker.
	1193, Frank Haseks.
1200, Pacroak...............June 20	
	1211, M. Dvorak.
1214, Mraz ....May 20	
1215, Kula ....June 21	
1221.......................May 22	
	1292, *Frank Stengl*, cigars.
1329, Slade ....May 12	
	1447, F. Marek.

Twenty-first Court.

506, Wastlewstsky ....April 30	560, *John Fink*, cigarmaker.
	563, Frank Kolar.
	565, Frank Roth.
576, Christofek...............May 18	
585, Polprok ....June 26	
596.......................June 7	625, F. Kodack.

Twenty-fifth Place.

	63, Kadou, home finisher.
	125, M. Ribik, custom tailor.
	149, Mrs. Martin, shirt maker.
	149, Mrs. Fuchs, shirt maker.
205 ....April 12	

Twenty-fifth Place—Concluded.

Small-Pox.

242, Irving....................May 11

Tenement House Shop.

233, Mrs. Watsick, shirt maker.
239. V. Sherry.

599, E. Locust, custom tailor.

West Twenty-second Street.

750......................March 19
796, Werner................June 14
821..........................May 29

1037..........................June 4
1402, Merkonowski...........May 15
1582......................April 22
1616..........................May 23
1636, Randa, 5 cases........May 23

725, Somas.
748, G. Wandersee, custom tailor.

997, J. Slapak.
1026. *Peter Fuerts*, cigars.

1636, Anton Randa, custom tailor for Kelley Bros., 268
S. State st.

West Twenty-fifth Street.

25........................April 22

172, Kellihar..............May 24
174, Oakland...............May 24
210, Carey.................June 18

273.......................April 24
375..........................June 7
377, Wicke.................May 13
377, Ruffhagen.............June 6

508.......................April 24

529, Miehlke...............May 25

537, Larek.................April 30
538, Vicha.................April 30
546, Blood..................May 7
564.......................April 22

573, Stroedel.............April 26
584..........................May 29
586, Gienowitz.............May 29
601, Vemlichek............April 30
660........................April 24
660, Saukub.................May 10
603..........................June 8
1270, Eiland...............May 10

41, John Kadlec, custom tailor.

226, Mrs. Furst, shirts.

410, Mrs. Sullivan, shirts.
445, James Martin.
505, J. Vlack.

523, Mrs. Mattias, shirts.
524, J. Wullin.
526, Mrs. Furcht, shirts.
528, Mrs. Kolat, shirts.

530, Charles Kircleous.

546, Mrs. Movatch, shirts.

565, Mrs. Richards, finisher.
572, V. Jeran, custom tailor.

Van Horn Street—(Beginning at Laflin Street).

625, Joseph Marzek.
625, F. Malcrac.
625, J. Kristle.
632, Mrs. Proskok, shirts.
633, Mrs. Filip, shirts.
640, Mrs. Barash, home finisher.
640, Annie Jaroby, shirts.
643, Mrs. Hcabacka, shirts.
643, Mrs. Coonling, shirts.
682, A. Truska, custom tailor.
682, J. Fybecki, custom tailor.
687, Mrs. Winkelshoper, finisher.
688, Mrs. Varley, shirts.

Van Horn Street—Continued.

Small-Pox.

696.....................April 22
696, Kasik.................April 30
718, Burianek..............April 30
721, Manipaka..............June 9
770, Jonas.................April 27
771, Sewalska..............May 24
771, Barloblak.............June 16
773.......................April 22
774.......................April 24
797, Schmitt...............April 27
801, Youscha...............April 27
801, Two cases.............May 8
801.......................June 9
802.......................April 24
803.......................June 6
897.......................April 22
907,......................April 24
918,......................April 22
927, Wessel................May 12
941, Vartouek..............May 12
947,......................April 22
953,......................May 4
974, Adler.................June 18
998,......................April 22
998,......................May 4

Tenement House Shop.

696, T. Tylecki, custom tailor, working for John Hassar, 226 S. Halsted st.
696, Joseph Roklop, cigars.
703, Mrs. Dziadul, cloaks.
711, J. Dusek.
711, Frank Gratzek, shirts.
722, Mrs. Adams, home finisher.
734, Mary Kriracek, shirts.
745, Frank Fiala, shirts.
745, John Filip, custom tailor.
748, Mrs. Prochaska, shirts.
748, Joseph Prochaska, shirts.
748, Annie Prochaska, shirts.
755, Mrs. Wischnewska, home finisher.
763, Joseph Masek.
766, John Pecing.
784, A. Fenzel.
799, Mrs. Slumetzka, shirts.
802, Frank Maisher, shirts.
906, M. Dongilla.
907, Mrs. Seymauek, home finisher.
911, Mrs. Kienarovska, home finisher.
913, Strewpleska, home finisher.
922, Konehan, home finisher.
922, Knickert, home finisher.
923, Annie Hardenska, home finisher.
925, Mrs. Tuma, home finisher.
927, Frances Ostrowska, home finisher for Chas. Marquardt, 955 Hinman st., a contractor for Kohn Bros., 144 Market st., C. P. Kellogg & Co., 144 Market st., and L. C. Wachsmuth & Co., 122 Market st.
928, Mary Betraus, home finisher.
932, Mrs. Sauer, home finisher.
932, Mrs. Kessler, home finisher.
934, K. Pasaic, home finisher.
935, Mrs. Keydrowsky, home finisher.
940, Chas. Krojicek, cigars.
941, Mrs. Hoffmann, home finisher for W. Franz, 927 W. 17th st., contractor for Kuh, Nathan & Fischer, cor. VanBuren and Franklin sts.
944, Mrs. Cuse, home finisher.
944, Mrs. Lux, home finisher.
945, Mrs. Jerabek, home finisher.
945, Lizzie Taraba, home finisher.
947, M. Tarcaba, home finisher for W. Franz, 927 W. 17th st., contractor for Kuh, Nathan & Fischer, cor. Franklin and VanBuren sts.
949, Mrs. Sikasa, home finisher.
952, J. Jelinek, custom tailor.
953, Mary Kakosczkova, home finisher for W. Franz, 927 W. 17th st , a contractor for Kuh, Nathan & Fischer, cor. Franklin and VanBuren sts.
954, Jos. Fikiesz.
950, Mrs. Kracinska, home finisher.
968, Mrs. A. Younger, home finisher.
970, Mrs. Schwartz, home finisher.
970, Mrs. Grutsky, home finisher.
970, Mrs. Nyberrick, home finisher.
981, F. Swoboda, sweater.
987, F. Prospal, home finisher.
987, Mary Baleika, finisher.
992, Frances Tauhern, home finisher.
992, Mrs. Buserbulb, home finisher.
996, James Kadic.

Van Horn Street—Concluded.

Small-Pox.	Tenement House Shop.
	1005, Mrs. Fautana, home finisher.
	1005, Mrs. Spinka, home finisher.
1007, Holuopek..............June 4	
1007, Holoupek, 2 cases.....June 15	
	1010, Chas. Opitz.
	1011, Peter Otto, pants-maker for Cahn, Wampold & Co., 204-210 Monroe st.
	1017, F. and A. Schlenisky, home finishers.
	1019, Mrs. Pewandopsky, shirts.
1021, ...June 27	
1025, ...April 12	
1040, ...April 22	1040, Mrs. Buskevek, home finisher for Peter Otto, 1011
1040, Buskevek..............June 21	Van Horn st., contractor for Cahn, Wampold & Co., 204-210 Monroe st.
	1042, Mrs. Sierc, home finisher.
1044, Kencel ....May 7	
	1052, Mrs. Beanke.
1059, Zietk................April 23	
1059, Merdi...............May 10	
	1060, Jos. Malek.
1062 ....April 22	
1066, Ticek..................May 21	
	1071. *John Balor*, cigars.
	4085. John Cezok.
	1085, *V. Kozan*, cigars.
	1090, *Jos. Dundr*, cigars.
	1090, F. Titilach, custom tailor.
	1090, Mrs. Marsher, home finisher.
	1092, Mrs. Doubek, home finisher.
	1105, F. Rost.
	1106, *Jos. Hlavak*, cigars.
	1113, *John Zajicek*, cigars.
1118, Novak ....May 17	1118, Chas, Peschek, coat-maker for Ederheimer, Stein & Co., cor., Market and Jackson sts.
1118, Novak ....May 28	1118, Josie Novak, shirt-maker for Seaman Bros., 244 Monroe st.
	1121, Chas. Wolf, home finisher.
1125, Buks ....May 17	
	1138, John Hansen.

South Wood Street.

800, Jischa, 2 cases..........April 27	
813, Novak ....June 20	
	817, W. Wilkovsky.
	843, Mrs. Mandol, home finisher.
851 ....May 24	
856, Machy, 2 cases..........May 13	
	856, F. J. Dalezal, coatmaker for L. Loewenstein & Co., 122 Franklin st.

Wallace Place.

3, Williams..................May 24	
	6, Mrs. Kurofski, home finisher.
	8, J. Piderman.
9...................May 4	
	10, J. F. Novak, custom tailor.

Zion Place.

	14, John Zak.
20, Buhnba ....April 12	20, James Honota, contractor for Hirsch, Elson & Co., 160-162 Market st.
20, Schmitt ....April 28	
20 ....May 10	
26, Jongny..................May 12	
26, Kaughin ....May 18	
26, Vicheck................June 4	
	27, Jos. Houdrak.
	27, Mrs. Lismanski, home finisher.
	31, James Prepeschal.
35, Marvan..................April 30	
35, Marvan, 4 cases.........June 19	36, James Rades.
	39, M. Daisy, night finisher.